BODY ATLAS

by
STEVE PARKER
Consultant
DR KRISTINA ROUTH

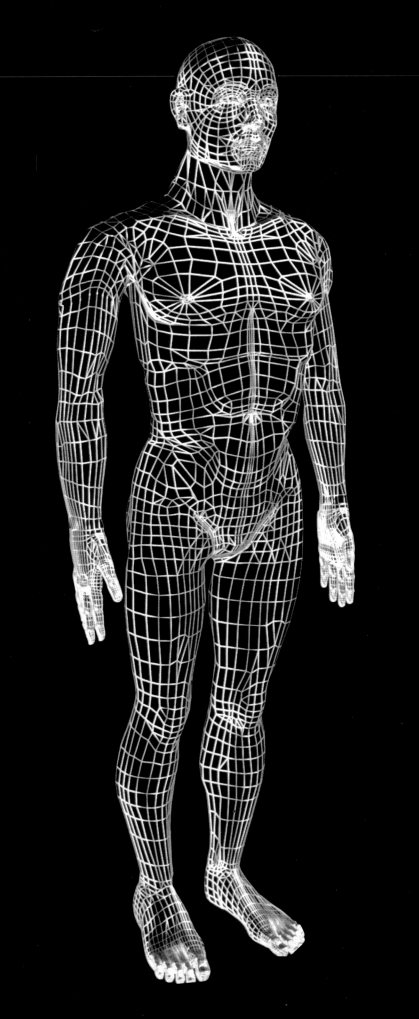

CONTENTS

HOW TO USE THIS BOOK

This book is your guide to yourself – an atlas of the human body. Follow the main text to get an informative overview of a particular area of the body, or use the boxes to jump to a specific area of interest. Finally, there are even experiments for you to try yourself!

Body Locator

The highlighted areas on the body locator tell you immediately which areas of the body you are learning about. This will help you to understand your body's geography.

Instant Facts

This box gives you snappy facts that summarise the topic in just a few sentences. Find out what the body's strongest muscle is, the longest bone, and much more.

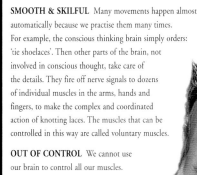

INSTANT FACT

When muscles are active they need up to ten times **the blood flow** to supply extra energy.

'Fast-twitch' muscle fibres can shorten and relax again in one-thirtieth of a second.

They are found in muscles that **make small, rapid movements**, like those which swivel the eyeball.

HEALTHWATCH

Cramp is when a muscle contracts powerfully for no reason and becomes tensed and hard. This can happen because of an awkward or uncomfortable posture, suddenly using muscles which have not been exercised, and more rarely, an underlying problem in the muscle's blood supply. The main remedy is to gently stretch and massage the affected area.

18

MUSCLES *In Control*

Muscles are controlled by the brain. It sends out signals along nerves to tell each muscle precisely when to contract. There are over 600 muscles in total, and the brain has to send out hundreds of signals every second.

SMOOTH & SKILFUL Many movements happen almost automatically because we practise them many times. For example, the conscious thinking brain simply orders: 'tie shoelaces'. Then other parts of the brain, not involved in conscious thought, take care of the details. They fire off nerve signals to dozens of individual muscles in the arms, hands and fingers, to make the complex and coordinated action of knotting laces. The muscles that can be controlled in this way are called voluntary muscles.

OUT OF CONTROL We cannot use our brain to control all our muscles. The muscles of the guts and other internal organs work in a different way. They are still under the control of the brain, but we cannot control them by willpower, no matter how hard we concentrate. They are called involuntary muscles.

JUST A TINY MOVEMENT OF A FEW MILLIMETRES can greatly alter a facial expression. We communicate using these muscles. Often a slight smile or fleeting frown can 'say' more than many words. However, extreme expressions are usually amusing – funny faces!

Healthwatch

Go here to read about illness and disease related to the relevant area of the body. For example, on the section about the skin, learn what damage the Sun can do to our cells, and what we can do to protect ourselves.

In Focus

This panel takes a really close look at one aspect of the human body, using stunningly detailed macro-imagery and stills taken from an anatomically correct digital model of human anatomy.

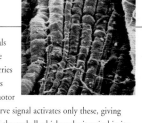

TO THE MUSCLES Nerves that carry signals to muscles are called motor nerves. The nerve branches near its end and each final 'twig' carries the nerve signals into a group of muscle fibres called a motor unit. In some muscles, each motor unit has fewer than 10 muscle fibres. One nerve signal activates only these, giving very precise control, as in the muscles behind the eyeball which make it swivel in its socket. In larger muscles such as those in the thigh, there may be more than 1,000 muscle fibres in a motor unit, and all contract together.

IN FOCUS
INTRICATE MUSCLE ACTION

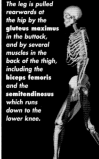

When walking, the leg is pulled forwards and up by the **rectus femoris** and **vastus muscles** at the front of the thigh, running from the hip to the knee. The **gastrocnemius** in the rear calf tenses to stop the ankle bending. The **biceps femoris** stabilizes the knee.

The leg is pulled rearwards at the hip by the **gluteus maximus** in the buttock, and by several muscles in the back of the thigh, including the **biceps femoris** and the **semitendinosus** which runs down to the lower knee.

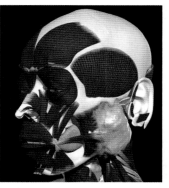

THE FACE CONTAINS MORE THAN 50 MUSCLES which give us our huge range of facial expressions. Some of these muscles are joined, not to bones, but to each other or to sheets of connective tissue.

Section Finder

This coloured panel cross-references with the contents page to tell you which section you are looking at.

 Diagrams

Go to this box for accurate scientific diagrams complete with annotations that tell you exactly what you are looking at.

 **TRY IT YOURSELF**

Eyebrows are lifted by the **frontalis** muscle under the forehead, and lowered and pulled together by the procerus muscle at the bridge of the nose. Look in a mirror while using these muscles. Try looking amazed (eyebrows highest) or annoyed (lowest).

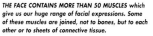

motor cortex

 MUSCLES ON THE BRAIN

The strip-shaped part of the brain that controls muscles is known as the motor cortex. Its different areas control muscles in various parts of the body. Those parts with very fine or precise control have larger areas of cortex. This diagram shows each part drawn in proportion to the area of cortex controlling its muscles.

Try it Yourself

This feature suggests activities for you to try. No special equipment is required – just your own body!

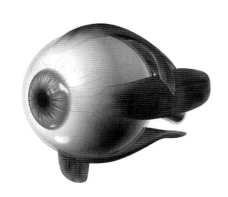

INTRODUCTION

Our body is an amazing place, a world that can be explored in the same way as the continents of the Earth. Just as our planet has different land forms, so our body has specific areas for doing certain tasks, each dependent on the other to keep functioning properly. This book is an atlas to the incredible world of the human body, from the outermost surface to the centre.

OUTSIDE TO INSIDE The story of our body starts with our skin, a tough surface that protects everything inside us. Everything that we see on the surface – the skin, hair and nails – is known as the integumentary system. Just underneath is another main body system – the muscles. The muscular system's task is to create motion, from the split-second blink of an eye to a sprint. However, muscles cannot work by themselves. They pull on bones to create movement. Bones make up the skeletal system which is at the body's core, a strong inner framework to hold up and support the many softer, floppy parts like blood vessels, nerves and guts. Since muscles and bones work together so closely, they are sometimes regarded as one system – the musculo-skeletal system.

CONTROL CENTRE While our skin, muscles and bones allow us to move around our environment, everything we do and feel is controlled by the most powerful and complicated part of the body system – the brain. Its workings are among the greatest challenges for scientists. Every year we learn more about the dozens of different parts inside the brain, and how they send nerve signals to and fro, millions of times every second. These nerve signals are the way we think, remember, decide, carry out actions and movements, have feelings and emotions, and understand. But the brain is so complicated that it seems the more we know, the more there is to find

The human body is covered with a tough but flexible layer of skin, which helps to protect us from damage.

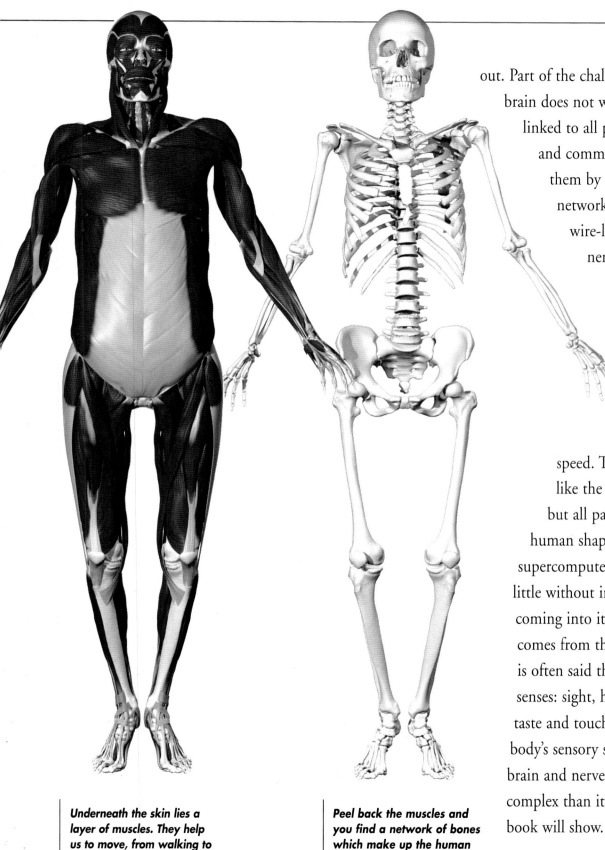

out. Part of the challenge is that the brain does not work by itself. It is linked to all parts of the body and communicates with them by an amazing network of branching, wire-like parts called nerves. These carry vast amounts of information to and from the brain, and all around the body, at incredible speed. The nerve system is like the global Internet, but all packed into one human shape. Like a supercomputer, the brain can do little without information coming into it. This information comes from the body's senses. It is often said that there are five senses: sight, hearing, smell, taste and touch. However, the body's sensory system, like the brain and nerves, is much more complex than it seems, as this book will show.

Underneath the skin lies a layer of muscles. They help us to move, from walking to carrying out complicated twists and turns.

Peel back the muscles and you find a network of bones which make up the human skeleton. It keeps everything together.

BREATHING AND BEATING In order to keep functioning, we must breathe every few seconds of every minute, every day – and all night too. The human body cannot last for a few minutes without taking in the substance oxygen, found in the air around us. Once the oxygen is inside the lungs, it must then spread all around the body, to every tiny nook and cranny. This is the job of the heart and blood. In the lungs, oxygen passes to the circulatory system. This consists of a central pump, the heart, the blood vessels or tubes that branch from it and the blood flowing through these vessels. Like breathing, the heartbeat is non-stop, day and night, year after year. Blood delivers around the body not only the all-important oxygen, but a host of other substances needed for life and health.

KEEPING IT GOING Food is the fuel we need to power everything we do from breathing to thinking. Food is processed by our digestive system – the part of the body that breaks down foods and absorbs liquids for the body's nutritional and water-balance needs. The system begins well above the abdomen, at the mouth. When chewed food is swallowed into the abdomen, it passes through the long digestive passageway of the stomach, small intestine and large intestine. What comes out of the other

THE HUMAN BRAIN IS THE MOST POWERFUL COMPUTER IN THE WORLD. Although it weighs just over a kilogram, it controls all of our thoughts and actions, and enables us to achieve great practical and creative feats.

end, at the base of the abdomen, is leftovers and unwanted material – one of several wastes that the body gets rid of every day. Another type of waste is removed by the urinary system. Its wastes are body byproducts and excess water filtered from the blood stream, as the liquid known as urine. This is stored in a stretchy bag, the bladder, until it is convenient for it to be expelled.

LONG-TERM SURVIVAL The final part of the body, the reproductive system, is not essential for the survival of an individual. But it is vital for the long-term survival of our kind – the human species. In a woman, the reproductive system is contained in the abdomen, but in the man, the parts are positioned below it. The 'product' of the reproductive process is a helpless bundle which alternately feeds and gets rid of waste, as well as crying and sleeping – a baby.

THE REPRODUCTIVE PARTS, OR ORGANS, make up the only body system which is not fully working at birth. The system becomes active 10–15 years later, at the time of life known as puberty.

IN CONTRAST TO THE RESPIRATORY SYSTEM, BLOOD CIRCULATION is the most widespread and far-reaching of all body systems. Its vessels branch around, into and through every body part.

The area of skin on a typical adult is **1.7 square metres** – slightly smaller than a single bed.

Skin is the body's heaviest single part, or organ, **with a weight of about 11 kg.**

Skin is thickest on the soles of the feet, **usually about 5 mm,** but thicker in people who walk barefoot.

👁 HEALTHWATCH

Most people have a few marks and spots on their skin, such as moles and freckles. These are usually harmless. But if such an area of skin changes in some way, it is wise to get medical advice promptly. Changes include colour, size, itchiness, bleeding, or becoming an open sore or ulcer. Rarely do these changes indicate a malignant (cancerous) growth, which can be treated most successfully in its earliest stages.

SKIN *ALL WRAPPED UP*

Your skin is far more than a simple covering to guard the body and provide protection from knocks and scrapes. It has a range of features and functions which warm you up when cold, cool you down when hot, and help you to feel the world around you.

AN ADAPTABLE SHIELD Skin continually rubs away due to wear and tear. But this 'living overcoat' also renews itself continuously to maintain its thickness so that the body is kept well protected. Our skin makes sure all our body's fluids and minerals, nutrients and other substances stay inside. It also keeps out water when we swim or laze in the bathtub.

A BABY'S SKIN has a fairly thick layer of 'padding' underneath it, called subcutaneous fat. This tends to reduce with age, and the skin itself also becomes thinner and more fragile, so it cuts more easily and takes longer to heal.

SELF-REPAIRING GERM BARRIER Skin prevents harmful microbes, called germs, from invading the internal parts. If it is damaged or wounded, it repairs itself to keep germs out and fluids in. In addition, skin is a barrier which stops harmful rays from damaging the body's insides. Ultra-violet (UV) rays produce the redness and pain of sunburn, while other rays carry heat which could dry out the delicate, moist inner parts.

HUMAN SKIN IS RARELY MORE THAN FIVE MILLIMETRES THICK, except perhaps on the soles of the feet. An elephant's skin is ten times thicker, at five centimetres, and in total can weigh as much as four adult people.

Magnified thousands of times, the skin's surface looks like the forbidding landscape of a far-off planet.

The loose skin flakes here are clumps of dead microscopic cells, ready to absorb wear and impact. They fall away when their task is done.

HOT & COLD Our skin plays a vital role in keeping the body's temperature within narrow limits. If the body is too hot, our skin reddens and sweats to encourage heat loss. When the body is chilled, our skin goes pale and its tiny hairs stand on end as goose-bumps or goose-pimples, to conserve warmth. Skin also provides one of the body's five main senses – touch. Our skin tells us not only if something is touching us, but also if that object is hard or soft, hot or cold. It also tells us is something is painful and damaging, helping us to protect ourselves against further harm.

SKIN BEGINS LIFE as soft and smooth as a baby's bottom. It gradually loses its softness and elastic nature with age, forming ridges and wrinkles around curves, at joints and where it is regularly stretched.

✋ TRY IT YOURSELF

Gently pinch a fold of skin from the back of your hand between thumb and forefinger. Assess the fold's thickness, and the skin itself is about half this thick. Try this on various body parts. Find areas where the skin is strongly attached to the underlying parts and cannot be lifted as a fold.

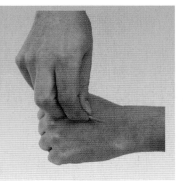

🔥 THE RULE OF NINTHS

If skin is burned in an accident, it may not only be very painful, but life-threatening due to fluid loss and risk of infection. Emergency medical workers use the 'rule of ninths' to assess the extent of the damage. If it exceeds 9% of the body, hospital treatment is vital.

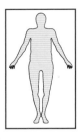

SKIN *UNDER THE SURFACE*

📖 INSTANT FACTS

A typical epidermal cell **lives for 3–4 weeks** before being rubbed off.

The **body loses an estimated 30,000** of these surface epidermal cells every second.

The body has about 2,000 million melanocyte cells, which produce the skin pigment (colouring) melanin.

On normal healthy skin, the numbers of germs such as bacteria per square cm **vary from 5,000** on the forearm, **to 200,000** on the forehead, more than one million on the scalp and up to **5 million in the armpits**.

Every month, there's a 'new you'! The entire outer surface of skin is replaced every four weeks. This tough upper layer protects the lower layer of skin, which is much more delicate and sensitive. You can feel this when you accidentally scrape off the upper layer in a graze, exposing the lower one – ouch!

MULTIPLY *&* DIE!

Your skin has two layers. The upper layer is called the epidermis and the lower layer, the dermis. The main task of the epidermis is protection. At the base, millions of microscopic cells multiply rapidly, producing billions of cells every hour. These cells pass upwards as multiplying produces yet more cells beneath. As the epidermal cells rise to the surface, they flatten out and fill with a tough substance, a protein called keratin.

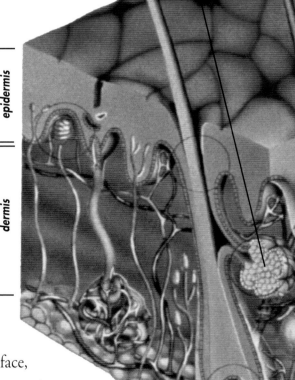

sebaceous gland

sweat pore

sweat gland

epidermis

dermis

hair follicle

🔬 UNDER THE SKIN

A cross-section of our skin shows the different layers clearly. The epidermis, dermis, collagen and elastin fibres and subcutenous fat layer appear throughout the body. The relative thickness of the epidermis and dermis vary greatly. In ordinary body skin the epidermis is ten times thinner. In skin thickened by rubbing, as on the foot sole or well-used hands, the two layers are almost equal.

👁 HEALTHWATCH

Skin is the most visible body part affected by illness. Invading germs cause infections such as measles, rubella and chicken-pox, usually recognized by the type of skin rash they produce. However the rash can vary from person to person, so medical help is needed to check the identification. The skin may also take on a yellow tinge in jaundice, which is usually due to a problem with the liver.

IN FOCUS
SKIN DISEASES

JUST BELOW The dermis is fixed to the base of the epidermis. This busy place is crammed full of tiny blood vessels and nerve endings that give us the sense of touch. The tiny blood vessels are capillaries. They bring nutrients and oxygen to the skin, so that it can keep replacing itself. Roots of hairs and the coiled micro-pipes of sweat glands also begin at the bottom of the dermis. Sweat glands pierce the epidermis above to open at the surface as sweat pores. Holding everything together are collagen fibres and elastin fibres. Collagen fibres give the skin its durable strength, while elastin fibres allow the skin to stretch and spring back as the body moves.

SKIN COLOUR IS DUE TO pigment-making cells called melanocytes. If skin is exposed to the Sun's UV rays, its melanocytes become more active and make the epidermis darker. This shields the underlying layers from UV, which could otherwise cause harm.

ONLY SKIN-DEEP Scattered through the base layer of the epidermis are cells called melanocytes. They make tiny grains of a dark substance called melanin. The grains pass into the surrounding epidermal cells and give these colour. Everyone has the same number of melanocyte cells in their skin. Differences in skin colour are determined by the levels of melanin produced by our skin. These amounts are mostly controlled by our genes.

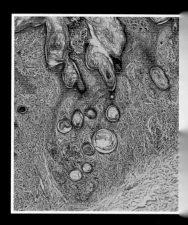

A malignant melanoma is a skin cancer caused by too much exposure to the Sun's harmful rays. It can be cut out during minor surgery.

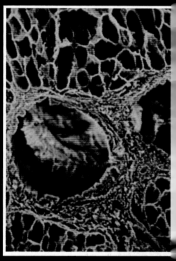

This is a birthmark caused by a dense collection of tiny blood vessels. Like many skin marks it can be removed by freezing the skin, known as cryosurgery.

blood vessels

subcutaneous fat layer

collagen and elastin fibres

🖐 TRY IT YOURSELF

Sweating helps us grip. Try picking up a small item like a paperclip. Then thoroughly wash and dry your hands and try again. Now that the thin film of sweat has gone, it's more difficult to get grip and hold tiny items.

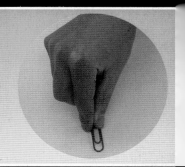

A typical adult with fair or blonde hair has about **130,000 hairs** on their head.

This number is less for other colours — about **110,000** for brown, **100,000** for black, and **90,000** for red or ginger head hairs.

A **head hair lasts for up to five years**, an eyebrow or eyelash hair for only 10 weeks.

Head hairs lengthen by about 3 mm each week, with fine fair hair growing at a slightly slower rate than thick, dark hair.

👁 HEALTHWATCH

Detectives like hair! It takes up tiny traces of substances passing through the body, including poisons such as the toxic metals mercury and arsenic. Also, like skin, hair indicates general health. If it grows slowly, thin and fragile, this may suggest a poor diet or generalized illness.

SKIN *Hairy Human*

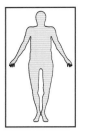

Most people have more hairs than a gorilla or a chimp – about 20 million in total. The reason we look much less hairy is that our body hairs are much shorter and thinner than ape hair. Early humans probably needed their hair to keep warm, but today hair is mainly something to trim, style, colour or remove.

IT'S A HAIR'S LIFE Hairs do not live for ever. In fact they hardly live at all. The base of a hair is called the root, and nestles inside a tiny pit in the skin called a hair follicle. Cells in the follicle multiply and add to the root. They fill with hard keratin, glue themselves together into a rod shape, and rapidly die. The rest of the hair, called the shaft, is gradually pushed upwards in the process. A single scalp hair grows like this for about three years. Then it falls out and the follicle rests for up to six months, before sprouting a new hair. Luckily, this natural replacement happens at different times all over the scalp, rather than all at once. About 100 old hairs are lost daily and 100 new ones appear.

TO SOME PEOPLE, HAIR IS A SELF-RENEWING FASHION ACCESSORY, to colour and style. But it does have uses. It offers some protection to the head against cold, heat, the Sun's ultra-violet rays and physical knocks.

IN FOCUS
HUMAN HAIR

APES SUCH AS ORANG-UTANS have fewer individual hairs than humans. However, their body hairs are much longer and thicker. The long hair helps rainwater to run off its body, in its tropical rainforest home.

SLIDING NAILS Like a hair, a fingernail or toenail has a root, under the skin at its base. The nail lengthens here and slides slowly along its under-layer with the finger, called the nail bed, towards its cut edge. Like hairs and epidermal skin, nails are made of the hard protein keratin. Nails may seem to have few uses, but a fingernail forms a firm support to prevent the soft, fleshy fingertip from flexing too much. This allows us to press and pick up small objects and gauge the finger's pushing force. Also, how would you scratch an itch if you didn't have any fingernails?

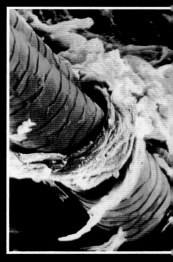

A hair is a scaly-looking cylinder of flattened, keratin-filled cells wrapped around an inner rod of longer cells.

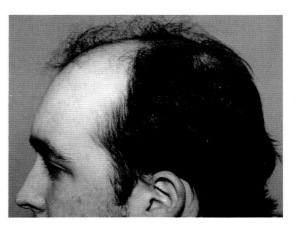

TREATMENTS FOR HAIR LOSS ARE ANNOUNCED REGULARLY, but a 'cure' has still not been found. Part of the reason for the typical 'baldness' of male-pattern hair loss is genetic. Another part is hormonal, caused by raised levels of the male hormone testosterone.

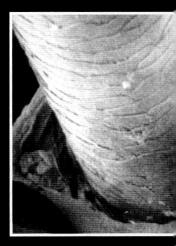

By the time a hair shaft is tall enough to emerge from its follicle, it is completely dead.

TRY IT YOURSELF

Hair is amazingly strong, with a tensile (pulling) strength greater than steel wire of the same thickness. Try to break a long scalp hair. Compare its strength to cotton thread, which is about 100 times thicker – which do you think is stronger?

HAIR FOLLICLES

A hair follicle is a pit in the epidermis that folds down into the dermis. Associated with the follicle are two important structures. One is the sebaceous gland, which makes the natural oils and waxes that keep our skin supple and water-repellent. The other is a tiny muscle, the arrector pili (erector papilla), which pulls the hair upright (see page 12-13).

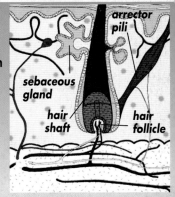

arrector pili

sebaceous gland

hair shaft

hair follicle

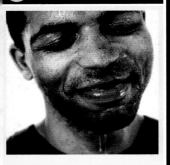
The body has about **three million sweat glands**.

If all their tiny tubes were straightened and joined, **they would stretch 50 kg**.

In normal conditions **the body produces one-third of a litre of sweat daily**.

An active body in hot conditions can lose more than **two or three litres of sweat through a day**.

HEALTHWATCH

Skin can ruin a holiday! Sudden exposure to ultra-violet rays in strong sunshine causes sunburn, where the skin turns red, swells and blisters. If the temperature gets too hot for our skin to keep our body cool, our body temperature rises and we get heat stroke. This causes confusion, cramps, and collapse. When the body gets too cold, we get hypothermia. Symptoms include intense shivering, paleness and collapse.

SKIN *Hot & Cold*

Helping to control body temperature is one of skin's most important tasks. It can change from a warmth-retaining 'overcoat' to a heat-losing 'radiator' in just a few minutes. The human body works best at a constant temperature of 37 degrees Celsius.

COOL IT? When our body temperature climbs above normal, the body has several ways to help us cool down. The small blood vessels carrying blood to the skin can change their width under control of nerve signals from the brain. When we are hot, they widen, sending more blood through the skin, making it reddened or flushed. This helps us cool down. When we are hot, we start to release more water, called sweat or perspiration, from tiny sweat glands in the skin. As this water dries it draws heat from the body. Finally the tiny muscles that control the position of the hairs spring into action to help us cool down. These muscles relax, making the skin hairs flatten, and helping heat to escape. Behavioural reactions kick in, too. We look for a cooler, shadier place, perhaps remove clothing, and fan ourselves too.

Sweat is about 97 per cent water, with salts containing minerals such as sodium. As these are lost in sweat, they must be replaced to maintain the balance of body fluids and minerals. This is why some sports drinks have minerals in them as well as water.

IN FOCUS
SWEATING

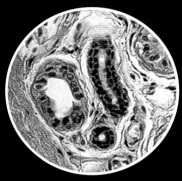

Sweat glands are curly tubes in the skin, here cut crossways. They pass through the dermis and open up onto the skin's surface as a sweat pore. On fingertips, sweat glands open along the skin ridges. Ink or powder sticks to this sweat film to outline the ridge pattern in a fingerprint.

Up to one-quarter of body warmth is lost from the head, face and neck. So a hat, hood and scarf, long hair, and for men a moustache and beard, all help to insulate the body in extra-cold conditions.

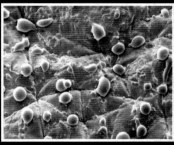

Sweat appears after we do exercise, get too hot or feel nervous and worried. This microscope picture shows sweat droplets (blue) lying on the skin surface, having emerged from the tiny holes called sweat pores.

WARMING UP If we get too cold, opposite reactions kick in. If body temperature is low, blood vessels narrow. Less blood flows to the skin, and this reduces loss of heat from skin to air. Less sweat is released from the sweat glands, and the muscles attached to each hair pulls the hair upright, helping to trap air near the skin and keep in heat. The muscles also make the skin around the hair pucker into a small mound. Lots of these mounds are known as goose-bumps or goose-pimples. Body muscles also shiver to generate warmth.

TRY IT YOURSELF

Put a clear plastic bag over your hand for a few minutes, loosely tied at the wrist. See how tiny water drops form inside the bag. These are from sweat which has evaporated from the skin, then condensed on the plastic. The skin is always releasing a small amount of sweat, called perspiration.

GOOSE-BUMPS

Each hair in the skin has a tiny muscle attached to it. When we feel cold, worried or frightened, the muscle pulls the hair, tilts it more upright, and also makes the skin around the hair heap up into a tiny hill called a goose-bump.

Most people have about **640 main muscles** involved in moving the whole body and its parts.

Depending on the amount of other **body tissues**, especially fat, the muscular system makes up about 45 per cent of an adult male body and 35 per cent of an adult female body.

The **biggest single muscle** is the *gluteus maximus* in the buttock, which pulls the thigh back at the hip when walking and leaping forwards.

The **smallest muscle is the *stapedius* deep in the ear**. It is thinner than cotton thread.

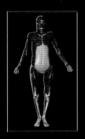

Working out in the gym, lifting weights and 'pumping iron' can't make your body develop more muscles, but it can make your muscles bigger. Each individual muscle is made of very thin muscle fibres, which can be expanded through exercise.

MAKING MOVEMENTS The muscular system is by far the body's heaviest and bulkiest system, forming about two-fifths of adult body weight. All of the body's hundreds of muscles work in the same basic way – they get shorter, or contract. But the movements range greatly in force and speed, from lifting a heavy weight to a tiny twitch of a finger.

SIZE *&* SHAPE The body has muscles of almost every shape. In the limbs many are the 'typical' spindle-like muscle shape, long and slim but wider and fleshy in the middle, which is called the muscle's body or belly. Some of the shoulder and hip muscles are triangular or rectangular, and others are branched like Vs, Ys or Ws. Those running alongside the backbone (spine) are strap-shaped, while muscles around the front of the lower body are sheet-like. Most muscles are joined at each end to bones, and move the body by pulling these bones. But some muscles are attached to other muscles, or to sheets of tough, strong connective tissue.

frontalis

masseter

deltoid

pectoralis

biceps brachii

digital flexors

rectus oblique

sartorius

rectus femoris

vastus lateralis

peroneus longus

soleus

🦵 MUSCLES

This view just under the skin shows the outermost or superficial muscles. Every one of the body's hundreds of muscles has a name. Also, every part of every major muscle has a name. Some muscles branch into two or more parts, called heads, which link to the same bones, or different ones. It's very complicated!

A LION HAS ALMOST EXACTLY THE SAME NUMBER OF MUSCLES AS A HUMAN. But many of these muscles are proportionally larger and more powerful, so that well over half of the big cat's bulk is muscle tissue.

Exercises such as press-ups show how our muscles work together to take the strain. During the pushing up part of a press-up, the **triceps brachii** muscle in the back of the upper arm takes much of the pressure.

The **semispinalis** and **splenius** muscles in the back of the neck keep the head steady.

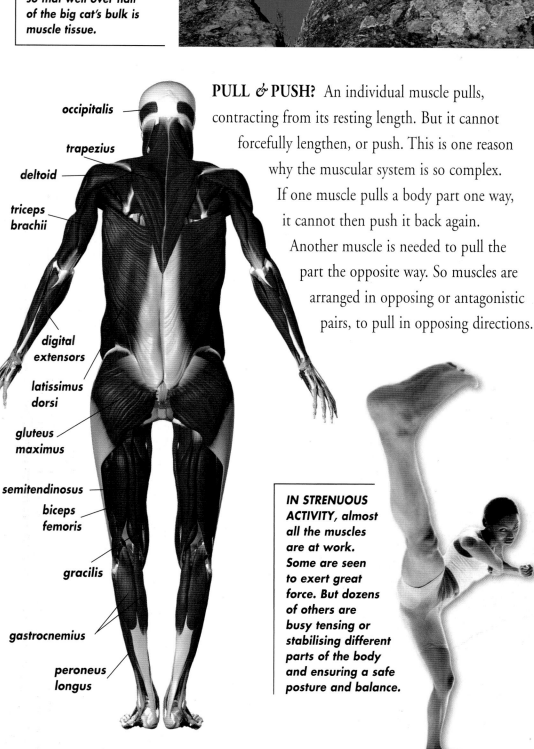

occipitalis
trapezius
deltoid
triceps brachii
digital extensors
latissimus dorsi
gluteus maximus
semitendinosus
biceps femoris
gracilis
gastrocnemius
peroneus longus

PULL & PUSH? An individual muscle pulls, contracting from its resting length. But it cannot forcefully lengthen, or push. This is one reason why the muscular system is so complex. If one muscle pulls a body part one way, it cannot then push it back again. Another muscle is needed to pull the part the opposite way. So muscles are arranged in opposing or antagonistic pairs, to pull in opposing directions.

IN STRENUOUS ACTIVITY, almost all the muscles are at work. Some are seen to exert great force. But dozens of others are busy tensing or stabilising different parts of the body and ensuring a safe posture and balance.

TRY IT YOURSELF

Tense your upper arm as though trying to bend the elbow, but without movement. See and feel with your other hand how the main elbow-bending muscle, the *biceps brachii*, bulges with the strain.

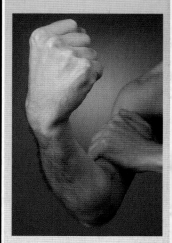

The shortest muscle fibres, **only 1 mm in length**, are in tiny muscles like the *stapedius* deep in the ear.

The longest muscle fibres, **over 30 cm**, are in the longest muscle, the *sartorius*. This runs down the thigh from the hip to the knee.

Most muscles can also be passively stretched to more than **twice their resting length**, when their opposing or antagonistic partner shortens.

HEALTHWATCH

A 'twinge' from a muscle may warn that a strain or tear is likely. A strained or 'pulled' muscle occurs when some of the muscle fibres are damaged and torn. The muscle still works but it swells and movement is limited, tender or painful. A ruptured muscle which has torn through so it cannot work at all is much more serious. This needs urgent medical attention.

MUSCLES *INSIDE A MUSCLE*

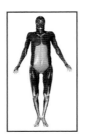

Whether a human body belongs to a thin and weedy weakling, a hunky power-lifting champion or a slim but strong and supple athlete, its 640-plus muscles all have the same inner structure and they all work in the same basic way.

MUSCLE FIBRES A single muscle is a collection of bundles of hair-thin threads known as muscle fibres or myofibres. They look like many electrical wires or optical fibres bundled together into a large communications cable. Most muscle fibres are between one and five centimetres long, and thinner than cotton thread. A large muscle has several thousand fibres, arranged in groups of 100-200. Each group is wrapped in a strong covering and called a fascicle. The whole muscle is contained in a tough but flexible outer covering called the epimysium.

MUSCLE FIBRILS Each muscle fibre is only as thick as a human hair. Yet inside it contains bundles of even thinner parts called muscle fibrils or myofibrils. And inside each fibril are bundles of still tinier thread-like parts, actin and myosin. To make a muscle contract, the actins and myosins slide past each other, and make the fibrils and fibres shorter.

TRY IT YOURSELF

Clench your fist looser then tighter. Watch the inside of the wrist. See the long tendons tightening under the skin. These connect the muscles in the forearm to the bones in the fingers and pull to curl the fingers.

A THIN LAYER OF BODY FAT UNDER THE SKIN ALLOWS WELL-DEVELOPED MUSCLES TO STAND OUT MORE CLEARLY.
The muscle at the angle or point of the shoulder is the deltoid. From it the triangle-shaped **pectoralis major** *slopes down to the lower centre of the chest. The 'six-pack' on the front of the abdomen is the* **rectus abdominis.**

IN FOCUS
SKELETAL MUSCLES

SOMEONE PULLING A TRUCK LIKE THIS HAS TO GRADUALLY WORK THEIR WAY DOWN THE ROPE.
The long, thin actins and myosins in a muscle move past each other in a similar way, to make the muscle contract.

CONTRACTION A typical muscle contracts mainly in its middle or belly region. This gets wider and bulges as the muscle becomes shorter, although the volume of the whole muscle is the same whether it is contracted or relaxed.

MUSCLE TO BONE Most muscles taper at each end into thinner, tougher, paler, rope-like parts called tendons. The tendon is 'glued' very strongly into the covering of the bone that the muscle moves. As the muscle contracts it pulls on the bone and moves it. However, many muscles can also pull without movement, as they take the strain to steady and stabilise body parts.

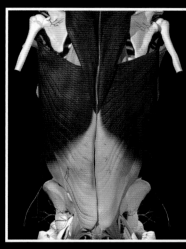

The muscles that help us to move are called striped or striated muscles. This is because under a microscope you can see bands or stripes. These are formed by the actins and myosins.

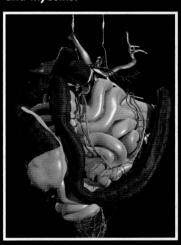

Muscles of inner organs like the intestines (above) are unstriped or unstriated. They have no microscopic bands.

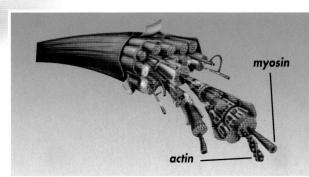

myosin

actin

INSIDE A MUSCLE

A muscle is a bundle of fibres, and each fibre is a group of fibrils. A single fibril contains threads of 'lumpy' myosins and 'frilly' actins. (One of each is shown at the bottom right.) These are the substances which slide past each other to shorten the muscle.

When muscles are active they need up to ten times **the blood flow** to supply extra energy.

'Fast-twitch' muscle fibres can shorten and relax again in one-thirtieth of a second.

They are found in muscles that **make small, rapid movements**, like those which swivel the eyeball.

HEALTHWATCH

Cramp is when a muscle contracts powerfully for no reason and becomes tensed and hard. This can happen because of an awkward or uncomfortable posture, suddenly using muscles which have not been exercised, and more rarely, an underlying problem in the muscle's blood supply. The main remedy is to gently stretch and massage the affected area.

MUSCLES In Control

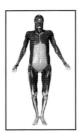

Muscles are controlled by the brain. It sends out signals along nerves to tell each muscle precisely when to contract. There are over 600 muscles in total, and the brain has to send out hundreds of signals every second.

SMOOTH & SKILFUL Many movements happen almost automatically because we practise them many times. For example, the conscious thinking brain simply orders: 'tie shoelaces'. Then other parts of the brain, not involved in conscious thought, take care of the details. They fire off nerve signals to dozens of individual muscles in the arms, hands and fingers, to make the complex and coordinated action of knotting laces. The muscles that can be controlled in this way are called voluntary muscles.

OUT OF CONTROL We cannot use our brain to control all our muscles. The muscles of the guts and other internal organs work in a different way. They are still under the control of the brain, but we cannot control them by willpower, no matter how hard we concentrate. They are called involuntary muscles.

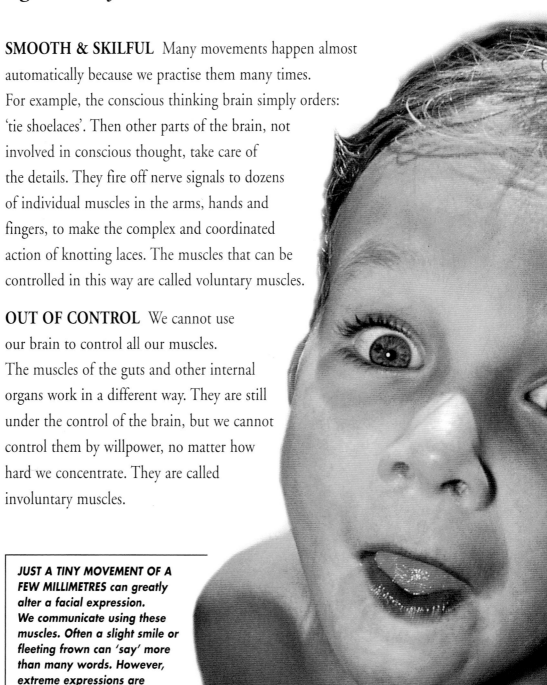

JUST A TINY MOVEMENT OF A FEW MILLIMETRES can greatly alter a facial expression. We communicate using these muscles. Often a slight smile or fleeting frown can 'say' more than many words. However, extreme expressions are usually amusing – funny faces!

IN FOCUS

INTRICATE MUSCLE ACTION

TO THE MUSCLES Nerves that carry signals to muscles are called motor nerves. The nerve branches near its end and each final 'twig' carries the nerve signals into a group of muscle fibres called a motor unit. In some muscles, each motor unit has fewer than 10 muscle fibres. One nerve signal activates only these, giving very precise control, as in the muscles behind the eyeball which make it swivel in its socket. In larger muscles such as those in the thigh, there may be more than 1,000 muscle fibres in a motor unit, and all contract together.

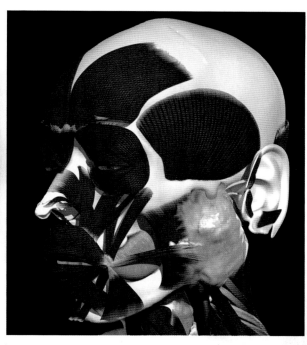

THE FACE CONTAINS MORE THAN 50 MUSCLES which give us our huge range of facial expressions. Some of these muscles are joined, not to bones, but to each other or to sheets of connective tissue.

*When walking, the leg is pulled forwards and up by the **rectus femoris** and **vastus** muscles at the front of the thigh, running from the hip to the knee. The **gastrocnemius** in the rear calf tenses to stop the ankle bending. The **biceps femoris** stabilizes the knee.*

*The leg is pulled rearwards at the hip by the **gluteus maximus** in the buttock, and by several muscles in the back of the thigh, including the **biceps femoris** and the **semitendinosus** which runs down to the lower knee.*

✋ TRY IT YOURSELF

Eyebrows are lifted by the *frontalis* muscle under the forehead, and lowered and pulled together by the *procerus* muscle at the bridge of the nose. Look in a mirror while using these muscles. Try looking amazed (eyebrows highest) or annoyed (lowest).

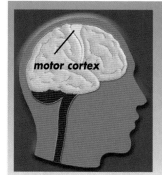

🧠 MUSCLES ON THE BRAIN

motor cortex

The strip-shaped part of the brain that controls muscles is known as the motor cortex. Its different areas control muscles in various parts of the body. Those parts with very fine or precise control have larger areas of cortex. This diagram shows each part drawn in proportion to the area of cortex controlling its muscles.

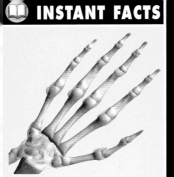
The skeleton makes up about **one-seventh of the body's total weight**.

The average number of **bones in a human skeleton is 206**.

These include **28 bones in the skull**, 26 in the backbone or spinal column, **32 in each arm** and hand, and 31 in each leg.

However, there are variations. About one person in 20 **has two extra ribs**, making 13 pairs instead of 12.

Three bones in the body are 'floating' and not directly joined to any other bone. These are the hyoid in the front of the neck, and the two kneecaps.

BONES *HUMAN SKYSCRAPER*

Old human bones in museum cases are usually white, rigid, flaky and dead. But bones inside the body are creamy-grey, slightly flexible, smooth-surfaced and very much alive.

KEEPING US TOGETHER Like the parts of a skyscraper, the bones form a strong inner framework that hold up softer parts like guts, nerves and blood vessels. All the bones together are known as the skeleton. They give height, shape, solidity and stability to our entire body.

LIVING LEVERS Our skeleton not only supports the rest of our body, it also helps us move. Bones are pulled by muscles and so move body parts. In particular, the body has many examples of 'living levers', especially in the arms and legs. For example, the elbow is bent by the biceps muscle in the upper arm. This shortens by just a few centimetres. But its lower end is attached to the forearm very near the elbow. So the forearm bone works as a lever to make the movement larger. Near the elbow the forearm bone moves just a couple of centimetres, pulled by the biceps muscle. But at its other end, attached to the wrist and hand, it moves up to 50 centimetres.

collarbone (clavicle)

shoulder blade (scapula)

humerus

breastbone (sternum)

radius

ulna

wrist bones (carpals)

finger bones (phalanges)

fibula

shinbone (tibia)

ankle bones (tarsals)

The arms and legs have a similar arrangement of bones. There is one in the upper part (upper arm and thigh), two in the lower part, a cluster of smaller bones in the wrist and ankle, and five sets making up the fingers and toes.

HEALTHWATCH

Healthy bones need a regular supply of various minerals, especially calcium. This is very important for babies and children, whose bones are still growing. Calcium-rich foods include milk and other dairy produce, eggs, green leafy vegetables, beans and peas, nuts and shellfish.

skull

jawbone (mandible)

HUMANS HAVE AN INTERNAL OR ENDO-SKELETON, surrounded by muscles and other parts. Animals like crabs and beetles have an outer or exo-skeleton, forming a hard external case with the muscles and other parts inside.

hipbone (pelvis)

thighbone (femur)

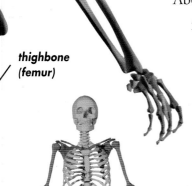

kneecap (patella)

foot bones (metatarsals)

toe bones (phalanges)

ABLE PROTECTION In addition to the twin aims of support and movement, the skeleton also protects our inner organs. Most noticeable is the upper dome of the skull which forms a strong, rigid casket around the delicate brain. About seven bones on each side of the upper face form a bowl-shaped cavity, the orbit (eye socket), in which the eyeball nestles. The upper backbone (spine), ribs and breastbone create a flexi-cage around the heart and lungs, which shields them from physical damage but also allows breathing movements.

TWO-PART SKELETON

There are two main parts to the whole skeleton. One is the central support or 'spine' down the middle of the body and it consists of the skull, face and jaws, backbone, ribs and breastbone. It is known as the axial skeleton and contains 80 bones. The other part, the appendicular skeleton, contains the 126 bones making up the parts that 'hang off' the axial skeleton. These are the limbs – the shoulders, arms, hands and fingers, and the legs, ankles, feet and toes.

● Axial Skeleton ● Appendicular Skeleton

TRY IT YOURSELF

Most bones are covered by skin, connective tissue and layers of fat and muscles. But here and there we can feel a bone just under the thin skin. The point of the elbow is the end of the main forearm bone, the ulna. The hard lumps on the ankle are not ankle bones, but the lower end corners of the lower leg bones, the tibia on the inside and fibula on the outside.

At the start of a sit-up, muscles relax and most bones lie flat.

The neck muscles tilt the head at the set of seven neck backbones. Stomach muscles bend the lower backbones and tilt the hip bones.

The hip joints allow the whole backbone to swing upright.

The body's **longest bone** is the thigh bone or femur.

The largest and broadest is the hip bone or pelvis. **It is made of six parts** firmly joined in a C shape. The lowest part of the backbone, called the sacrum, fits into the C's gap.

The **smallest bone is the stirrup** (stapes) deep inside the ear, which is involved in hearing. it is hardly larger than this letter U.

The **strongest bone for its size** is the lower jaw or mandible.

BONES *BONES GALORE*

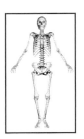

Each bone is an amazing example of strength combined with lightness. Bones are perfectly designed for muscles to attach to, and can withstand powerful pulling and pushing forces.

SHAPES AS CLUES Almost every bone in the body has a different shape. Even pairs of bones, such as the thigh bones, are not identical. However, bones can be divided by shape into several main groups, which give clues to the way the bones work inside the body.

LONG & SHORT
The main bones in the limbs are long and slim. They work like girders to give the limb its lever-like action, when the legs walk or the arms reach out to grip. The ends of a long bone are widened to give a larger surface area where they join their neighbours. However, the main length or shaft is narrow to save weight but maintain strength. Short bones are smaller and found mainly in the spinal column or backbone, wrists and ankles. They have less flexible joints than

The ribs form a bendy cage around the delicate lungs and vitally-beating heart. Each rib bone is slim and also springy, almost like tough plastic. So it can usually bend slightly if it suffers a hard knock, rather than snap and damage the lungs.

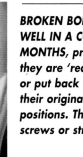

BROKEN BONES USUALLY HEAL WELL IN A COUPLE OF MONTHS, *provided they are 'reduced' or put back into their original positions. They may need holding with pins, screws or strips until the parts knit together.*

their neighbours. But these bones usually occur in groups so the flexibility adds up from one to the next. Flat bones include the shoulder blades and hip bones, which provide large surface areas for limb muscle attachments.

INSIDE A BONE A typical long bone has three layers. On the outside is a 'shell' of hard or compact bone, which is extremely strong and dense. Inside this is a honeycomb-like layer called spongy or cancellous bone, which has lots of bubble-like space to save weight. In the middle of the bone is the marrow, which looks like yellow or pink jelly. This makes microscopic cells for the blood.

Protective equipment is vital during physical action, especially when moving fast as in cycling, or when sports players impact at high speeds. The skull makes a strong natural casing for the brain. But a helmet is a very helpful 'second skull' around the body's most important part.

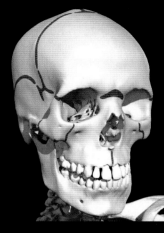

The large upper dome of the skull is called the cranium. It has eight bones – the biggest is the frontal bone under the forehead.

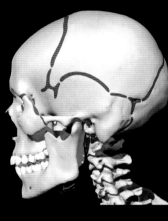

The main bones at the side of the skull are the parietal higher up, and the temporal bone below it. A hole in the lower middle of the temporal bone leads to the inner ear. The ring-like neck bones are called cervical vertebrae.

Bones contains many minerals and nutrients – enough to feed an active carnivore like the leopard. Bone minerals include calcium, magnesium, phosphate, carbonate and fluoride. The bone marrow has plenty of iron and energy stored as fat.

 TRY IT YOURSELF

Human bodies vary in proportions, especially in the lengths of the arms, legs and main body. Usually the femur, or thigh bone, makes up about one-quarter of adult height. But this proportion is less in a young person. The length of the foot, from toe to heel, is typically one-sixth of overall height. How do you measure up?

 MICRO-BONE

A bone may seem solid. But really it is made of microscopic, tube-shaped units called osteons. In the centre of each osteon is a tunnel (dark hole) for nerves and blood vessels. Around it are cylinder-shaped layers, one within the next, like the rings inside a tree. The small, dark, spider-like shapes are bone-making cells, osteocytes.

Bone is one of the **strongest known materials**, for its weight.

If the skeleton was made of steel, it would weigh almost **five times as much**.

Bone is also strong under compression or squeezing force – **three times more so than glass**. It tends to 'give' and absorb some of the force, **unlike concrete, which cracks**.

HEALTHWATCH

The mineral calcium is needed for muscle contraction. If a person's food contains little calcium, the body 'borrows' it from bones, making them weaker and more likely to split or crack. In osteoporosis the slow but constant renewal of bone becomes out of balance. Old bone tissue is broken down faster than new bone tissue is produced, so bones become thinner and weaker. This affects most older people to some extent, especially women. But it is less marked in people who exercise regularly through life.

BONES *Busy Bones*

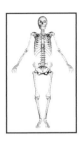

Bones not only support, move and protect. They make 'new blood', act as stores of minerals in emergencies and even change shape slightly as they adapt to stresses and strains placed on them.

WET BONES Each of our bones contain about one-fifth water, which means the whole skeleton of an adult contains more than two litres of water. Bones are attached to many other parts. They are linked to muscles by tendons, and at joints with other bones by ligaments. Bones also have blood and nerve supplies, just like other body parts.

THIRSTY WORK Our bones use lots of energy and nutrients. These arrive along blood vessels, which pass through small holes in the outer layer of hard bone to reach the interior and marrow. The blood flowing back out of the bone takes away new microscopic cells produced by the marrow, to replace cells which wear out and die as part of natural body maintenance. The blood cells include both oxygen-carrying red cells and disease-fighting white cells, made by the skeleton at the rate of three million every second!

TRY IT YOURSELF

Bone is a lot less bendy than cartilage. Put your thumb on the end of your nose and wiggle it around. Then try the same on the bridge of the nose (bone).

IN FOCUS
NERVOUS BONES

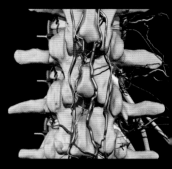

Every bone has a complex web of nerves to sense any problems, and blood vessels to keep it supplied with nourishment and take away waste products. Here are the nerves (yellow) and small veins (blue) on the vertebral bones of the backbone, seen from the rear.

A BIG BREAK Bones have nerves which, like blood vessels, pass through small holes into the interior. Some of these nerves tell us whether a bone is bending too much or suffering from infection. If a bone has broken, the pain we experience is very sharp and severe. If certain bones are put under great stress regularly, the bone material itself grows thicker and denser in the parts which cope with the stresses. This is known as remodelling. It changes the shape of the bone slightly and helps the skeleton as a whole to deal with the physical forces involved. If our bones are not kept active, however, they become weak and brittle. Then, when they are suddenly put under extra stress – snap!

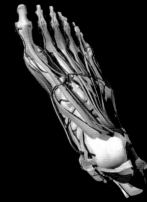

Even a tough body part that we stand, walk and run on every day has many inner pieces. The main sole of the foot is supported by metatarsal bones, with intricate sets of muscles, nerves, arteries (red) and veins.

SPACE'S WEIGHTLESS OR ZERO-G (no-gravity) conditions mean that the skeleton is under very little strain or pressure. Astronauts do exercises to put pressure on their bones and keep them strong.

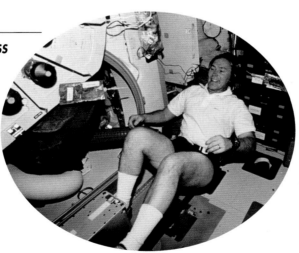

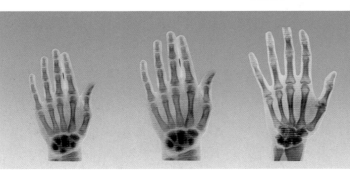

OSSIFICATION

As bones develop in the growing body, they are not actually made of bone at first. They form as cartilage (a tough, elastic tissue) or gristle. Gradually the cartilage hardens and becomes true bone, in a process called ossification. The wrist 'bones' are not fully ossified until the teenage years.

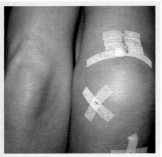
The **largest single joint** in the body is the knee. Two knuckle-shaped ends on the thigh bone fit into shallow dishes in the top of the shin bone.

As the knee straightens, **the bones twist slightly** to 'lock' the joint and make the leg rigid from hip to ankle.

The knee also has its **own special protection** at the front — the kneecap bone, or patella.

'Arthritis' is a general term for pain, swelling and inflammation in a joint. There are many different kinds of this problem. In osteoarthritis the cartilage covering the bones becomes cracked and pitted, making movements limited and painful. In rheumatoid arthritis, the body defences mistakenly attack various parts, including joints. The synovial membrane becomes swollen and the joint is reddened, stiff, tender and painful.

BONES *Twists & Turns*

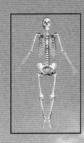

A joint is where two bones meet. Joints allow the body to bend and move in many different ways. There are hundreds of joints in your body. Without them, your skeleton would be so rigid you wouldn't be able to move at all.

INSIDE A JOINT Most joints allow movement. They are encased in a bag-like part, called a synovial membrane. This makes a slippery liquid called synovial fluid which, like oil in a car engine, lubricates the joint to reduce wear and tear. Around the synovial capsule is a tougher bag, the joint capsule, which helps to stop the bones coming apart.

JOINT DESIGN The amount of movement a joint can make varies hugely. The knee lets the lower leg swing forwards and backwards, like a hinge, but not to either side. In the backbone, each joint between two neighbouring bones (vertebrae) has a flexible cushion-like pad inside, the intervertebral disc. The two bones tilt slightly on this, with limited movement. But over the whole backbone the movements add up so the back can bend almost double.

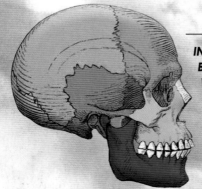

IF A JOINT IS FLEXED TOO FAR, it becomes uncomfortable or painful. However, regular careful exercise makes a joint gradually more supple, so it can go through its full natural range of movement without discomfort.

IN A SUTURE JOINT THE BONES ARE FIRST JOINED WITH FIBRES, and then grow and knit together into one rigid structure. All that remains is a faint wiggly line, as in these skull sutures.

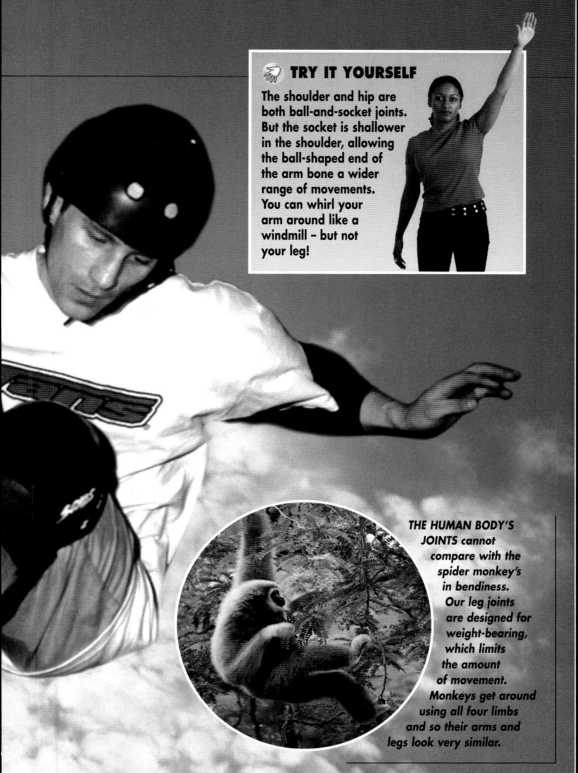

👉 TRY IT YOURSELF

The shoulder and hip are both ball-and-socket joints. But the socket is shallower in the shoulder, allowing the ball-shaped end of the arm bone a wider range of movements. You can whirl your arm around like a windmill – but not your leg!

THE HUMAN BODY'S JOINTS cannot compare with the spider monkey's in bendiness. Our leg joints are designed for weight-bearing, which limits the amount of movement. Monkeys get around using all four limbs and so their arms and legs look very similar.

🦵 INSIDE THE KNEE

The knuckle-like lower ends of the thigh bone (shown here in rear view) are covered by shiny cartilage. The ligaments around and within the joint (white cords) are stretchy or elastic and prevent it from over-flexing. If the bones slip and come out of their normal positions, this is a dislocation.

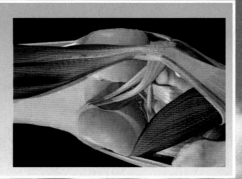

IN FOCUS
JOINTS IN ACTION

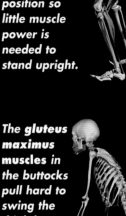

As the body lowers the front and back thigh muscles steady and balance the weight over the hip joints. The knees 'lock' in the straight position so little muscle power is needed to stand upright.

The **gluteus maximus muscles** in the buttocks pull hard to swing the thigh bone down and back at the hip joint. The lower thigh muscles pull on the knee joint.

Sitting down happens mainly at the hips and knees. The back and hip bones stay upright. The top of the thigh swivels in its ball-and-socket joint to form a right-angle with the hip bone.

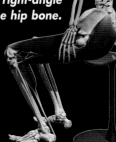

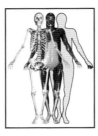

Running speeds become slower the further we go. The lungs reach their maximum supply of oxygen needed to 'burn' blood glucose for energy. **The heart has a maximum pumping rate** to supply fresh blood to the muscles and to remove their waste products such as **lactic acid**.

---

100 metres – **less than 9.8 seconds** – 10.2 metres per second.

42,195 metres (marathon) – **less than 2 hours, 5 minutes** – 5.6 metres per second.

ALL TOGETHER *FULL SPEED AHEAD*

In a race against the animal kingdom, even a world-record human runner would be well down the list of fastest movers. But imagine the contest broadened to several events, from sprint to marathon, and even swimming. Then the human body's all-round moving ability might begin to win through.

IN THE WATER, FISH ARE FASTEST *reaching speeds of more than 30 metres per second. Humans achieve over 2 metres per second in sprint swims, using mainly arm power.*

ARMS & LEGS One reason for our adaptable movement is that our arms and legs are different. Most mammals have four similar limbs designed for weight-bearing, walking, running and jumping. Our legs carry out these actions, while our arms have a wider range of movement and are free for other tasks, such as balancing the body on a narrow beam or hanging from a rope or bar. Also, most wild animals

HUMAN *The fastest humans sprint at more than 11 metres per second, but only for a couple of hundred metres. The arms assist the legs by pumping like pendulums to give added momentum for each stride. Over 1,000 metres the speed falls to nearer 7 metres per second.*

RHINO *The fastest large sprinter is probably the rhinoceros. At up to two tonnes, it weighs almost 30 times more than an average person. Yet it can pound along faster, at a peak speed of more than 13 metres per second. So it's unwise to try and outpace a charging rhino.*

can swim in a basic fashion to save their lives. But humans have devised several swimming strokes powered mainly by the arms.

BRAIN *&* **BODY** Our muscle, bone and joint systems work as amazingly complex and coordinated teams, even in common activities such as walking or eating. Hundreds of muscles pull on bones and flex or stabilise joints. But part of our wide-ranging capacity for different movements is due, not to the body itself, but the way it is controlled by the brain. Our large brains allow us to work out the best way to carry out a certain movement, to learn and practise and refine this many times. As athletes and sport-players know, we use our intelligence and concentration to make a movement gradually more effective and efficient. Animals can learn too, but in a much simpler way, and only when they need to, as a matter of survival. In a ten-event Olympic Games between the humans and the animals – who do you think might win?

 TRY IT YOURSELF
The world record for long-jump is almost 9 metres. Try measuring this outside or in a large room. How near could you get to it? The high-jump record is nearly 2.5 metres. Measure this as well, although you may need to go outside again because the ceilings in most homes are too low! These records show the incredible feats set by the fittest, best-trained human bodies.

OSTRICH *The heaviest bird is perhaps more comparable with a human, rather than the cheetah, since it moves on two legs not four. The ostrich races at almost 20 metres per second for a short distance, and can maintain up to 10 metres per second for several kilometres.*

CHEETAH *The cheetah is the fastest of all runners, reaching almost 30 metres per second. It has long, rangy limbs and a flexible back which arches up and down to increase its stride. But after half a minute this African big cat sprinter is all but exhausted.*

People who are 'nervous' are jumpy and edgy, slightly worried and tense. But in one way, everyone is nervous all the time. The body's nerves are always working, carrying astonishing amounts of information in the form of tiny electrical pulses called nerve signals.

THREE PARTS IN ONE

The nervous system is really three systems combined into one. The largest part of the entire nerve network is the brain. The base of the brain joins to the body's main nerve, the spinal cord, which runs down the inside of the neck and back. The brain and spinal cord together are called the central nervous system. This is because they are central to the way the system works, in the way that a central computer controls many devices and machines attached to it.

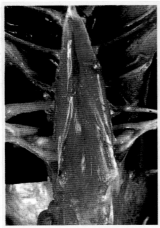

If all the body's nerves were joined end to end **they would stretch about 100 km**.

The thickest main nerve is the **sciatic nerve in the hip and thigh**, which is as wide as your thumb.

The longest nerve is the tibial nerve, which runs from above the knee almost down to the ankle.

A place where several nerves come together and branch again in **a small network is called a plexus**.

👁 HEALTHWATCH

Lack of some vitamins and minerals in our diet can cause nerves to stop working properly. These include the vitamins B1, B6, B12 and E, and the minerals calcium, potassium, sodium and magnesium.

EVERY SECOND THE BRAIN TAKES IN HUGE AMOUNTS OF INFORMATION from the senses and sends out millions of signals to control the body's hundreds of muscles. This is why we sometimes have to concentrate really hard to complete difficult tasks, such as jet skiing or other sports.

SUPPORT SYSTEMS The second part of the nerve network is known as the peripheral nervous system. It is made up of all the nerves that branch from the brain and spinal cord out to various parts of the head and body. The third part of the nerve network is called the autonomic nerve system. It is made up of areas inside the brain and spinal cord, and other nerves that run down the back, on either side of the spinal cord, and into body parts like the lungs, guts and heart. The autonomic nerve system controls processes that happen automatically, without us thinking about them. These include digesting food and making the heart beat.

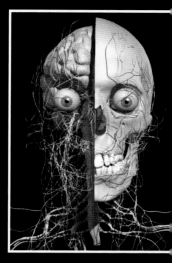

An intricate network of small nerves links the brain to the muscles and skin of the head and face. These are among the body's most touch-sensitive parts with precise muscle control.

NERVES ARE SOME OF THE BODY'S MOST DELICATE, EASILY-HARMED PARTS. *Neurosurgeons are doctors who specialize in operations on the brain and nerves, dealing with single nerve fibres that are thinner than human hairs.*

TRY IT YOURSELF

Have you felt the tingling sensation of 'pins and needles', after sitting awkwardly, or applying pressure on part of the body? This feeling warns that a nerve is being squashed, or the blood vessels bringing blood to it are being squeezed. Next time you get this feeling, move, stretch, exercise and rub the part as soon as possible to feel better.

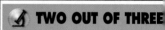

TWO OUT OF THREE

The central nervous system is the brain's main control centre. The peripheral nervous system carries nerve impulses between the central nervous system and other parts of our body.

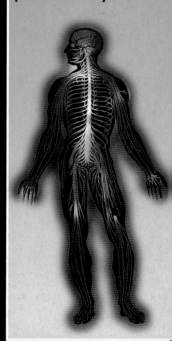

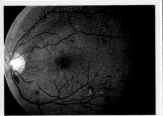
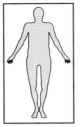

A single nerve signal lasts for 1/700th of a second.

Most nerve fibres can **carry up to 300 nerve signals per second.**

The fastest nerve signals travel at more than **200 metres per second,** so they can go from toe to brain in less than 1/100th of a second.

The slowest signals travel at **less than one metre per second.**

NERVES *ALL ABOUT OUR NERVES*

Most parts of the body are repaired and replaced as they gradually wear away. The skin renews itself every month, and the inside of the stomach is replaced every three days. But nerves are different. They are so complicated that they rarely get repaired or renewed.

NERVE CELLS Inside every nerve, there are thousands of tiny thread-like fibres of microscopic nerve cells. The whole nervous system contains hundreds of billions of these complicated little cells. They carry tiny electrical signals, just like the wires inside a computer.

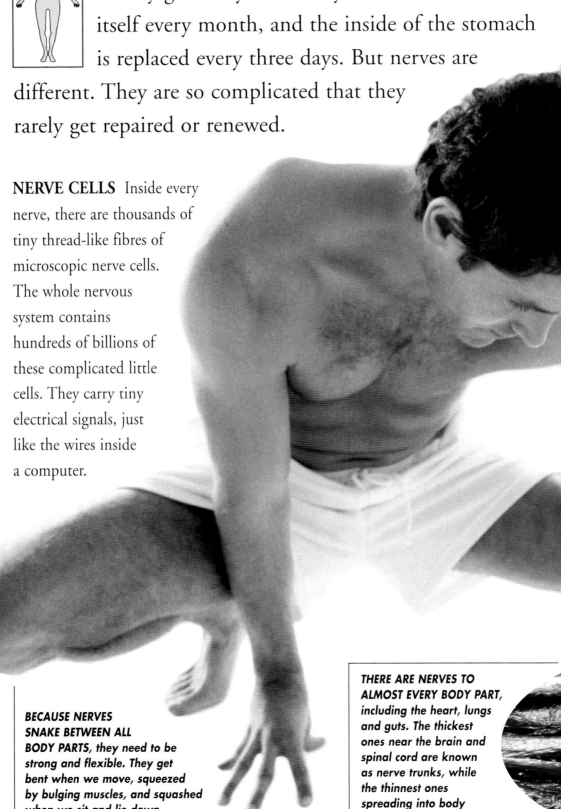

BECAUSE NERVES SNAKE BETWEEN ALL BODY PARTS, they need to be strong and flexible. They get bent when we move, squeezed by bulging muscles, and squashed when we sit and lie down.

THERE ARE NERVES TO ALMOST EVERY BODY PART, including the heart, lungs and guts. The thickest ones near the brain and spinal cord are known as nerve trunks, while the thinnest ones spreading into body parts are terminal fibres.

IN FOCUS
NERVE CELLS

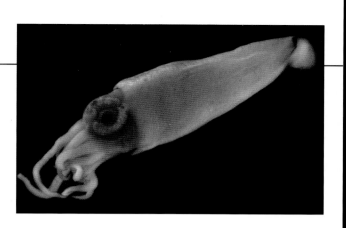

THE NERVE FIBRES IN THE HUMAN BODY are less than 1/1000th of one millimetre wide. In a squid, they are thicker than human hairs. Studying squid nerves has helped greatly to understand our own nervous system!

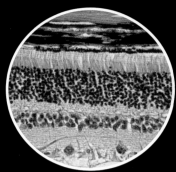

The ends of a nerve fibre are separated from other nerve cells by slight gaps called synapses. Electrical nerve signals 'jump' across these gaps in the form of natural body chemicals called neurotransmitters.

COMING & GOING On its own, a single nerve cell is not special. It simply passes on signals to other nerve cells. Linked together, however, these cells create something quite amazing. Each nerve cell receives signals from thousands of other cells, and passes on signals to thousands more. The numbers of different pathways for signals through the whole system, with billions of nerve cells, is almost endless. And every day, as we make decisions, imagine new thoughts, carry out actions and form memories, the pathways change.

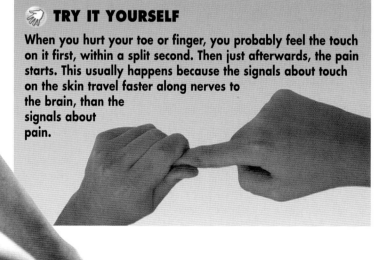

TRY IT YOURSELF

When you hurt your toe or finger, you probably feel the touch on it first, within a split second. Then just afterwards, the pain starts. This usually happens because the signals about touch on the skin travel faster along nerves to the brain, than the signals about pain.

Each nerve cell has many spider-like 'wires' called dendrites. These receive nerve signals and lead to a main cell body. The very long fibre or axon is like a wire. It carries the signals along and passes them to other nerve cells, at junctions called synapses.

FASCICLES

The nerve's strong outer covering, the epineurium, contains bundles of nerve fibres, each fibre being too thin to see. The bundles, called fascicles, are surrounded by 'padding' to cushion the fibres as they bend and twist with body movements. Each fascicle encloses up to 200 nerve fibres.

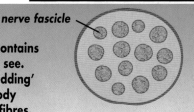

nerve fascicle

The average adult human **brain weighs 1,400 grams**.

It has more than **100 billion nerve cells**.

In normal health, there is **no link between brain size and intelligence** or cleverness.

Women have slightly larger brains in proportion to their body size, compared to men.

A new baby's brain is ⅓ of its adult size.

⊙ HEALTHWATCH

Most people get occasional headaches. However, a person who develops a severe headache together with a stiff neck, aversion to bright lights and perhaps a skin rash, may have the serious infection of meningitis. This is swelling and pain in the meninges, which are wrap-around layers covering the brain. Meningitis needs medical attention without delay.

BRAIN DRIVING FORCE

The brain looks like a lump of pinky-grey jelly. Despite its appearance, however, the brain is the place where we carry out mental processes, like thinking, remembering, feeling sensations and controlling our muscles. Surprisingly, however, the brain has no senses or muscles of its own.

AUTO-CONTROL The large, rounded, wrinkled part on top of the brain is called the cerebrum. One of the most important parts that lie underneath is the brain stem, which lies between the cerebrum and the spinal cord. The main job of the brain stem is to control automatic body processes. These include controlling the heartbeat, digesting food in the guts, overseeing our breathing, and keeping the body at a constant warm temperature.

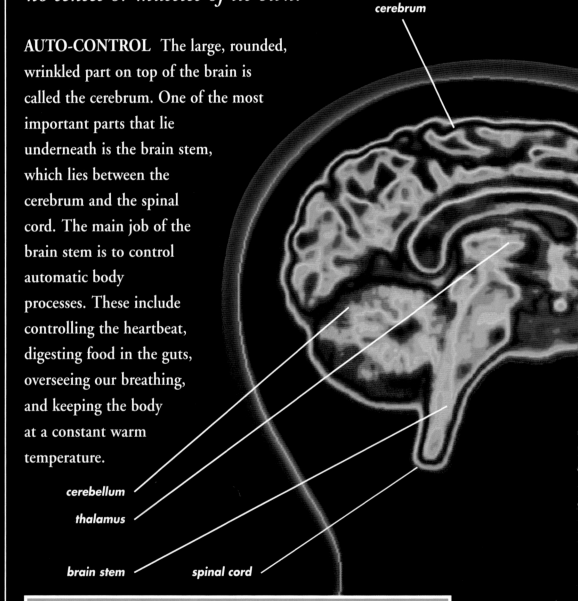

cerebrum

cerebellum

thalamus

brain stem

spinal cord

✔ BRAIN PARTS

This computer-generated graphic of a human brain shows the major parts, surrounded by the protective skull. The cerebrum is the area that controls most of our actions.

MAKING MOVEMENTS The lower rearmost part of the brain consists of another rounded, wrinkled part called the cerebellum. This makes up about one-tenth of the brain's total size, and controls the movement of our muscles. Nerve signals are sent down from the cerebrum to the cerebellum. Here the details of which muscles should tighten, and by how much, and for how long are worked out. This information helps the muscles work together as a team to make our movements smooth and precise.

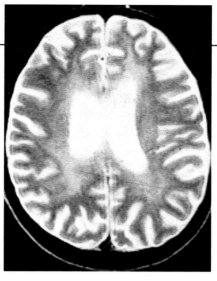

MRI (Magnetic Resonance Imaging) scans (above) show the details of the brain's inner structure, including its many blood vessels. These scans help to find problems such as lack of blood flow to part of the brain, which can cause the disorder known as a stroke.

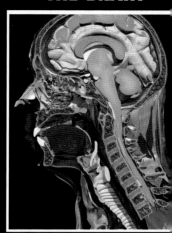

In the middle of the brain is a system of flattened hollow chambers called cerebral ventricles. They contain the same liquid that bathes the outside of the brain, known as cerebrospinal fluid.

MILLIONS OF NERVE SIGNALS FLASH AROUND THE BRAIN EVERY SECOND. These tiny electrical pulses can be detected by sensor pads on the skin of the head. The pulses are shown on a screen or paper strip as an EEG, electro-encephalogram. They show how the brain works and reveal disorders such as epilepsy.

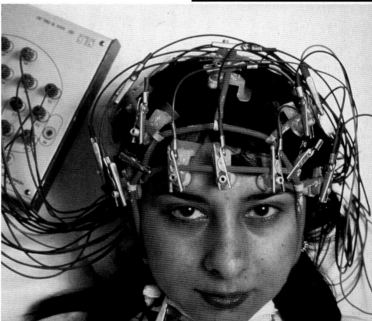

🖐 TRY IT YOURSELF

Gently tap the top of your head. It makes a dull thud. This is because underneath the skull, the brain is surrounded by a thin layer of liquid called cerebrospinal fluid. As the head twists and moves rapidly, or gets knocked, the fluid makes a moving cushion to protect the brain from damage.

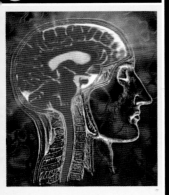
The outer layer or cortex of the brain, **spread out flat, would cover the area of a pillowcase**.

It contains **more than 50 billion nerve cells**.

Each of these nerve cells can have **connections with up to a quarter of a million other nerve cells**.

These **nerve cells give the cortex a greyish colour**, which is why the brain is sometimes called 'grey matter'.

👁 HEALTHWATCH

The brain is well protected by the skull, and during risky activities it should also be guarded by a hard-hat, helmet or similar headgear. But sometimes a blow on the head shakes it so much the person becomes unconscious – concussed or 'knocked out'. If this happens, no matter how brief, medical attention is needed to prevent later problems.

BRAIN Centres & Control

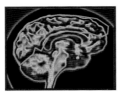

The mission control room at a space centre is full of people, screens and computers. Some plan the rocket's route, some receive information from the equipment on board, while others look after the fuel and engines. The brain inside your head works just like a complicated mission control room.

THE BODY'S MISSION CONTROL Over three-quarters of the brain is made up of the cerebrum. Its outer layer is called the cerebral cortex. This part of the brain acts as the body's 'mission control room'. The cerebral cortex is the main place where thinking happens, and where information is received from the senses, and sent out to the muscles. Like a control room, the cerebral cortex is highly organised. Different parts of the cortex, called centres, each deal with different jobs.

THE TWO SIDES OF THE BRAIN LOOK SIMILAR. *But in most people they have slightly different roles. The left side takes the lead for step-by-step thoughts, reasoning, dealing with numbers and facts. The right side is more active in awareness of shapes, colours, musical sounds and artistic skills.*

THE CEREBRUM HAS A VERY DEEP GROOVE ALONG THE MIDDLE FROM FRONT TO BACK, *dividing it into two cerebral hemispheres. More deep grooves divide each hemisphere into five main sections or lobes.*

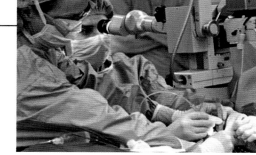

The brain has no sense of touch or pain. During surgery, it cannot feel the surgeon's cutting scalpels or laser beams. However, the brain coverings, or meninges, are very sensitive.

CENTRES FOR SENSES The lower part of the cortex is called the visual centre because it helps to control the sense of sight. Nerve signals arrive here from the eyes, and are processed and compared with information about scenes and objects already stored in the memory. The body's auditory (hearing) centre can be found on the sides of the brain. There is also a centre for taste (gustatory centre), and a touch centre, which runs in a strip from side to side, arching over the top of the brain.

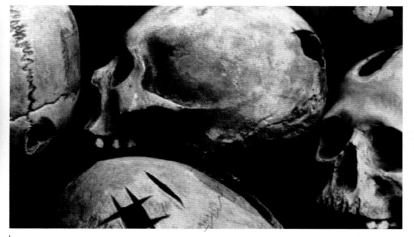

Archaeologists have found the skulls of people with holes drilled through them. Experts think these holes were made in an attempt to cure terrible headaches or release 'demons'. Remarkably, archaeologists can tell patients often survived this procedure, as lots of skulls with healed bone have been unearthed.

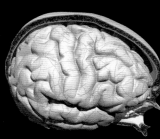

The upper front of each cerebral hemisphere is known as the frontal lobe. The frontal cortex covering it is important in what we call 'personality', and in the awareness of the body's position in its surroundings, so we don't bump into things!

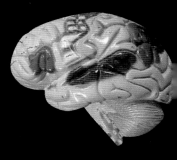

This coloured 'map' of the cortex shows the various centres for planning movements (very pale yellow) and making them (orange), touch on the skin (pale blue-grey), speech (blue), hearing (red) and vision at the brain's lower rear (dark yellow).

🖐 TRY IT YOURSELF

Can you write your name with your 'other' hand? Have a go. The first few tries will probably be terrible. Try 40 or 50 times, with short rests between. Compare the 50th attempt with the first. The motor centre in your brain has learned to control your hand and arm muscles to make a new pattern of movements.

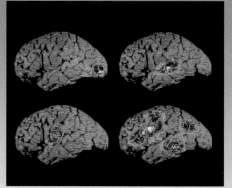

🖐 BUSY BRAIN

PET (positron emission tomography) scans show the brain's energy use and which regions are 'busiest'. This series of PET images shows the left side of the brain in a person who is staring (upper left), listening (upper right), speaking (lower left) and thinking about talking and moving (lower right).

BRAIN *LEARNING & MEMORY*

Can you remember your name? Your home address and phone number? The answer to these questions will probably be yes. What about the number of windows in your home? That might be more difficult.

Short-term memories last a few seconds or minutes. They are information we know we won't need to keep for long, like a little-used phone number before we call it.

Medium-term memories last a few hours or days, like what we ate during meals yesterday.

Long-term memories last many years, even a lifetime.

The life of any memory depends on how often it is 'refreshed' by thinking about it and recalling it regularly.

FINDING MEMORIES You might be able to answer the question about windows by using your memory in another way. In your imagination, go into a room in your house. You can see the windows in your 'mind's eye'. Count their number. Do this for each room, add up all the windows, and you have the answer. This shows how we remember not only names, faces, facts and places, and lessons we learn at school. We can recall scenes, feelings, smells, sounds and countless other memories.

SHORT & LONG No one really knows where this information is stored. A computer has a hard disc where it stores most of its information. But there is no single place like a 'hard disc' in the brain. Many brain parts work together to learn, make memories and then recall them. They include the outer layer of the cortex, and under it the thalamus, amygdala and hippocampus. A memory is probably a particular set of connections or pathways between the billions of nerve cells. Learning a new fact involves making a new set of connections.

OUR MEMORY FOR FACES IS ESPECIALLY AMAZING. *Some people can identify more than 100 faces from photographs, after seeing each one for just two seconds.*

IN FOCUS
CLEVER BRAIN

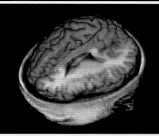

A part of the brain called the temporoparietal region helps the brain recognise true from false memories. In this PET scan, the red spot on the right shows that the brain is recognising a word that the person has heard before.

In this scan, the brain does not recognise the word that is being spoken, and so it is not active.

Take a card, any card ... Physical exercise and practise make muscles stronger and movements more skilled. In the mind, the same applies to memory. Mental exercise, using your memory and practising how to recall all help you to remember better and faster.

HIPPOCAMPUS

Short-term memories, like a quick text message, are based in the cortex of the brain. But these soon fade away unless they are important or remembered several times. The hippocampus seems to be important for making long-term memories that last weeks, months and years.

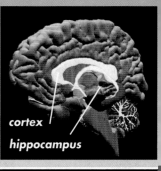

cortex

hippocampus

TRY IT YOURSELF

There are ways to improve your memory. These are called memory tricks. For example, use the first letters from the names of the items to make up a weird word. For this picture, it could be ...... This trick may seem difficult at first, but soon gets easier with practice.

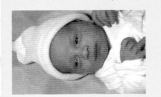
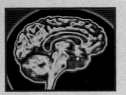

BRAIN *Wide Awake, Fast Asleep*

A newborn baby probably sleeps for 20 hours out of every 24.

Most **10-year-old children need about 10 hours** of sleep nightly.

Adults usually need 7–8 hours of sleep each night.

Some people are best with more than eight hours of sleep while others make do with six or less.

If a person is **deprived of a few hours' sleep**, then he or she 'catches up' on most of it over the next couple of sleep sessions.

It has been a long and exciting day. You have been wide awake, looking and learning, talking and listening. Yet five minutes after laying down in bed, you are fast asleep. But the brain is far from 'switched off'.

ALERT TO ASLEEP The part of the brain that controls our level of alertness is called the thalamus. Situated in the centre of the whole brain, it looks like two eggs side by side. The thalamus checks information coming in from the senses and the spinal cord, even when we sleep, to see whether it is important or not. If not, then it does not disturb the rest of the brain. But if there is a sudden loud noise, or a jolt, or perhaps a dangerous smell like smoke, the thalamus wakes up the rest of the brain.

UPS & DOWNS OF SLEEP Shortly after we fall asleep, the body becomes very relaxed. Our heartbeat, breathing and digestive system slow down. Most of our muscles become loose and floppy. This state is called deep sleep. About an hour later, our muscles start to twitch. Breathing becomes faster and shallower, and our eyes flick about, even though the eyelids stay closed. This state is called REM (rapid eye movement) sleep. After around 20 minutes, the body relaxes again into deep sleep. These changes from deep to REM sleep happen every hour or two through the night. The deep sleep gradually becomes lighter each time, until eventually we wake up.

OUR IMAGINATION SEEMS TO GO WILD IN DREAMS. Most people have several dreams each night, during REM sleep. But we usually remember a dream only if we wake up during or just after it. This illustration shows the famous writer Charles Dickens having a vivid dream.

Dolphins sleep with only one side of the brain at a time. The other side stays alert, receiving information from the eyes and other senses. If danger approaches the dolphin can react quickly without having to wake up.

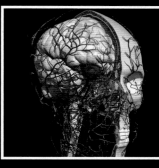

Many body parts have a much reduced blood supply during sleep. But the brain requires as much blood as when awake, supplied by the carotid arteries.

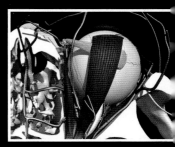

Several sets of muscles become active during REM sleep. Limbs twitch, lips quiver, and of course the six strap-like extra-ocular muscles behind each eyeball produce the eye movements.

WHY DO WE YAWN? No one really knows. It may be to get some fresher air into the lungs after slow, shallow breathing. It may be to exercise the face muscles, which encourages more blood to flow to them and to the brain as well.

THE THALAMUS IS IMPORTANT IN LEVELS OF ALERTNESS OR CONSCIOUSNESS, from very excited and 'buzzing' to deeply asleep. Exactly why we sleep is still not clear. The brain could be sorting out the events of the day, storing important information as memories and getting rid of the rest.

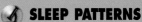

awake
drowsy
stage 1
stage 2
delta sleep
rem sleep

SLEEP PATTERNS

During sleep the nerve cells of the brain are still active. This is shown by the pattern of the brain's electrical signals while asleep. Shortly after we fall asleep we are very relaxed, but become more anxious during certain periods of sleep.

 ## TRY IT YOURSELF

Some nights we just cannot get to sleep. This is not a problem if it happens now and again. It helps to be not too hot, not too cold, and not too stuffy with some fresh air. If thoughts keep racing through your mind, try to think of peaceful places and happy times like holidays and relaxing in the sun by the sea, with the waves gently lapping on the shore, swish, swish ... zzzzzz.

More than half of the knowledge and memories in the brain come in through the eyes, as written words, pictures, diagrams and scenes. Each eye detects light rays and their patterns of brightness, colour and movement, and changes these into patterns of nerve signals for the brain.

An eyeball is almost a perfect sphere, measuring 24 mm across and the same from front to back, and 23.5 mm from top to bottom.

People with short sight (myopia) tend to have **bigger eyeballs**, about 28–29 mm.

People with long sight (hypermetropia) usually have **smaller eyeballs**, around 20–21 mm.

PICKING UP LIGHT

The eyeball has a white outer covering or sclera. At the front is the coloured iris. It has a hole in the middle called the pupil, where light rays shine into the eye. These rays pass through the clear jelly inside the eyeball and hit the retina. The retina contains more than 120 million microscopic cells called rods and cones. Each of these cells sends nerve signals when light rays hit it. The rods work well in dim light but see only shades of grey, from almost white to almost black. The cones work only in bright light but they see colours and details.

 HEALTHWATCH

Eyes are so precious that they need great care. Visors, goggles and similar protection shield them against injury and flying particles. These can be darkened when the eyes are at risk from too much light, like bright sunshine, glare off sand or snow, or the intense shine from equipment such as welding torches. A regular visit to the optician is also important. Looking into the eye can detect problems so they can be treated before they become serious.

THE IRIS CAN BE BLUE, GREEN, GREY OR BROWN depending on the amount of melanin in the iris. Blue eyes have the least melanin and are more sensitive to light.

✂ AROUND THE EYE

Arching over the top of the front of the eyeball is the lachrymal gland, which makes tears. Around the sides and rear are six small, ribbon-shaped muscles which swivel the eyeball in its socket. The socket is padded with soft fat for smooth movement.

EYELIDS PROTECT THE EYE FROM TOO MUCH LIGHT by automatically squinting. They close instantly if something comes too close to your eye. Every time you blink cleansing tears containing germ fighting chemicals clean your eyes and stop them from drying out.

ALL ANIMALS HAVE TEARS, BUT ONLY HUMANS CRY WHEN THEY ARE UNHAPPY OR HURT. Emotional tears aren't like the ones that are used to clean your eyeball when you blink, they are made up of different chemicals. No one knows why your body produces emotional tears, but when you are sad it can make you feel better to have a good cry.

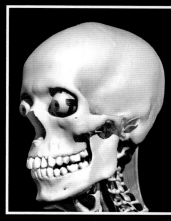

The eyes are almost forward outgrowths of the brain, expanded at the front into ball shapes which detect light. Each nestles well protected by skull bones in the orbit (eye socket).

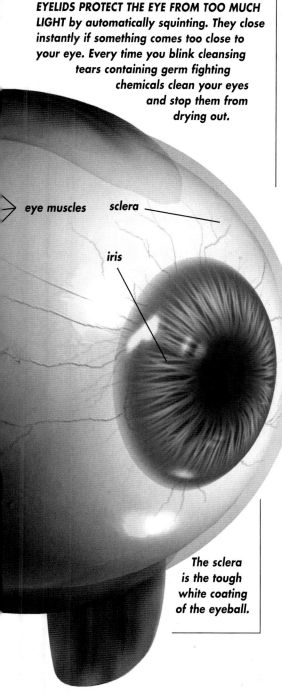

eye muscles   sclera

iris

The sclera is the tough white coating of the eyeball.

NEAR & FAR How can we judge if objects are near or far away? Each eye moves up, down and side to side by six small, strap-like muscles behind it. Stretch sensors in the muscles signal to the brain about the angle at which the eye looks. If both eyes look at a nearby object, they point inwards slightly. The more they angle inwards, the nearer the object, and the sensors detect this. There are also stretch sensors in the muscle which adjusts the thickness of the lens. The lens becomes thick to focus on nearer objects clearly, and thin for faraway ones. We also compare sizes of objects we know, and how colours and details fade as they get farther away, to judge distance.

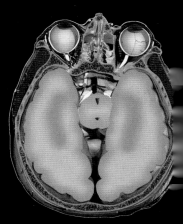

A cutaway across the middle of the head shows the short, stalk-like optic nerve connecting each eye to the brain. This nerve is by far the most complex sensory nerve, containing more than one million message-carrying fibres

THERE ARE THREE DIFFERENT KINDS OF CONE CELLS IN YOUR RETINA. They detect red, blue and green. Light stimulates different combinations of these cones to produce all the different colours you see. In some people one or more of their groups of cones are missing or do not work properly. They may get the colours red and green mixed up or even see things just in black and white and green. This is called colourblindness.

TRY IT YOURSELF

The brain takes cues from images received from the eyes to help it interpret what is being seen. Occasionally these images can trick the brain. Which of the two vertical line segments is longer? Although your visual system tells you that the right one is longer, they are equal in length.

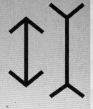

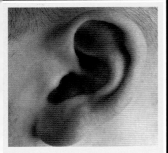
On the scale of pitch (high or low frequency), **ears can detect sounds from 25 to 20,000 vibrations per second.** Dogs can detect much deeper and much higher sounds than this.

On the decibel scale of volume, sounds **over 95 dB can harm our ears,** especially if they go on too long. That includes very loud talking, building work and aircraft noise.

The area of the brain that analyses nerve signals representing sounds is called the auditory cortex.

HEALTHWATCH

Ears look tough on the outside, but are very delicate inside. Sometimes germs get into the ear and a sticky fluid, mucus, collects. It causes earache and stops the eardrum or bones from moving freely. Poking things into the ear cannot help, and may be harmful. The problem needs a check by a doctor.

SENSES *EARS & HEARING*

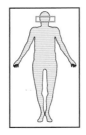

It's amazing how the mind can 'shut out' sounds. As you read these words, concentrating on vision, your ears are hearing noises around you. Yet your brain tends to ignore them – unless there's a sudden strange sound, or you hear your name.

INTO THE EAR HOLE When sound waves hit our ears, they go into the hole in the middle of the ear flap, on the side of the head. Across the end of this tunnel is a flap of skin, the eardrum. It shakes or vibrates as the waves hit. Attached to the eardrum are a chain of three tiny bones called the hammer, anvil and stirrup. (These bones were given their names long ago, when blacksmiths and horses were more common than today!)

SOME SOUNDS ARE TOO LOUD FOR OUR EARS. We put hands over our ears so we do not deafen ourselves!

TRY IT YOURSELF

Even if you close your eyes, you can usually hear the direction of a sound from one side – because you have two ears. The sound waves reach the nearer ear about 1/1,300th of a second before the other ear. They are louder in the nearer ear too. The brain detects these differences and works out the sound's direction. But try tilting your head to one side, so your ears point up and down – can you tell a sound's direction then?

IN FOCUS
COCHLEA

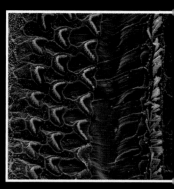

Inside each cochlea are more than 20,000 tiny hair cells, each with 50–100 even tinier hairs. The outer hair cells are arranged in three rows and the hairs on each one form a V or U pattern.

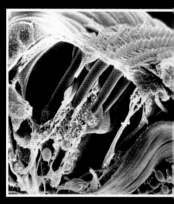

The hair cells (red) have a tall, column-like shape. Their hairs, known as stereocilia (yellow), do not project freely into the fluid in the cochlea. They are loosely embedded in an arch-shaped layer, the tectorial membrane, which vibrates with sound waves.

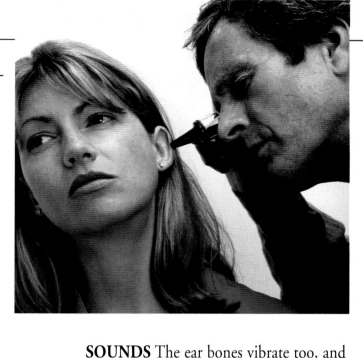

THE EAR TUBE OR CANAL HAS A LINING OF HAIRS AND STICKY WAX that traps bits of dust and dirt. As we speak and eat, jaw movements make the old wax loosen and move outwards, cleaning the tube naturally.

SOUNDS The ear bones vibrate too, and pass their movements to another part, called the cochlea. This is filled with liquid, shaped like a snail and about the size of a sugar cube. Inside, wound around its coil, is an incredibly delicate layer with thousands of microscopic cells that have even smaller hairs. The vibrations pass into the liquid and make these hairs vibrate too, which causes their cells to fire off nerve signals to the brain.

INNER EAR

The eardrum is about the size of the nail on the little finger – but thinner than this page of paper. It connects via the ear bones (ossicles) to the curly-shaped cochlea, which is only 9 mm across at its base and 5 mm tall.

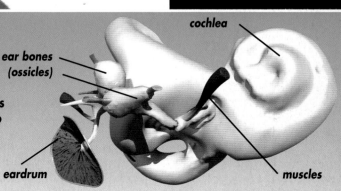

cochlea

ear bones (ossicles)

eardrum

muscles

The gravity sensors in the inner ear can **detect a change of position of less than one degree** (1/360th of a circle).

The nerve carrying balance information to the brain, **the vestibular nerve, has about 19,000 nerve fibres**.

All over the body there are more than **one million stretch sensors** in the muscles, joints, skin and other parts.

Being whirled around on roller-coaster rides is fun. The movements confuse the sensors inside the ears as the liquid and crystal lumps slosh around. Staying still for a short time afterwards lets the giddiness fade. But some health problems, like Meniere's Disease, cause this giddiness all the time, so you feel as if you are spinning or falling even when lying still.

SENSES *BALANCING ACT*

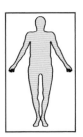

Balance is sometimes called the 'sixth sense'. However, it is not a sense in its own right. It is really a process which goes on all the time, involving various senses and many muscles. Even your eyes help you stay upright!

BALANCE AND THE EAR Every second, the brain receives millions of signals from all over the body, which it uses for the process of balance and staying upright. Many signals come from deep in each ear, near the part involved in hearing, the cochlea. Liquid-filled chambers next to the cochlea have tiny lumps of crystals in them. These hang down by the pull of gravity or swing around with head movements. The lumps pull on nerves which send signals to the brain about the head's position and motion.

JUST AS WE CAN LEARN TO READ OR WRITE, WE CAN LEARN TO BALANCE BETTER. Tiny stretch sensors in muscles and joints allow us to 'feel' the position and posture of body parts. This is known as the proprioceptive sense.

ABOUT TWO-THIRDS OF ASTRONAUTS BECOME 'SPACESICK'. There is no gravity to pull on the position sensors inside the ears. So there are no clues to being upright or upside down. In fact, in space there is no up or down.

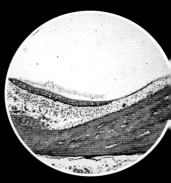

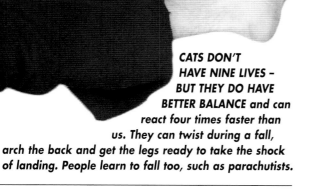

CATS DON'T HAVE NINE LIVES – BUT THEY DO HAVE BETTER BALANCE and can react four times faster than us. They can twist during a fall, arch the back and get the legs ready to take the shock of landing. People learn to fall too, such as parachutists.

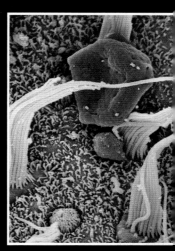

The macula is a patch of hair cells in a fluid-filled chamber next to the cochlea. Their tiny hairs are embedded in a thin layer of jelly-like crystals.

SWIRLING AROUND Deep in the ear are a set of three C-shaped tubes – the semicircular canals. Near the end of each tube is another tiny lump, which also pulls on nerve endings as the liquid in the tube swirls around with the head movements. There are also micro-sensors inside muscles and joints all over the body. These tell the brain the positions of joints and whether our muscles are flexed or not. The sensors tell you where your arms, fingers, legs and feet are! Finally, the skin of your feet feels pressure which varies as you lean different ways. This helps with balance too.

👆 TRY IT YOURSELF

Eyes are important for balance. Stand on one leg with eyes open. It should be fairly easy. Do the same with eyes closed. Without sight, you begin to wobble. Make sure you open your eyes again so you don't fall.

With the crystal layer removed the tiny hairs, stereocilia, can be seen as bundles sticking up from their hair cells. As the head moves, gravity pulls the crystal layer in different directions and bends the hairs making their cells send nerve signals to the brain

cochlea

semicircular canal

🩰 MADE FOR BALANCE

The main balance parts inside the ear are the semicircular canals, and behind them in this view, two chambers called the utricle and saccule. The canals sense head movements while the two chambers detect gravity and the position of the head by their maculae.

Most people can tell apart up to **10,000 different smells**, scents and odours.

One of the most **powerful smells is made by the chemicals called mercaptans**. These are present in skunk spray, and we can detect them at the tiny amounts of one part in 25 billion.

Some nerve signals for smell go to the parts of the brain dealing with emotions and memories, which is why some **smells bring back such strong feelings**.

HEALTHWATCH

Smell is an early warning system. We can smell many dangerous, harmful or poisonous substances. But some deadly fumes have no smell. They include carbon monoxide and carbon dioxide, made by certain forms of burning, such as vehicle engines. This is why vehicle engines should never run in an enclosed space like a garage.

SENSES *Nose & Smell*

Take a good sniff. There are almost certainly smells in the air around you. But maybe your nose and brain have got used to them. This is one of the many extraordinary features of the smelly sense.

SMELL PATCHES The nose's two holes are called the nostrils. They lead into twin air spaces called the nasal chambers. In the top of each chamber is an area of specialised lining about the size of a thumbnail. It is called the olfactory epithelium, or the smell patch. It has an astonishing 25 million tall, thin smell cells, packed together like the pile of a tiny carpet. Each of these smell cells has about 10 even smaller hairs called cilia, sticking down from it into the air space of the nasal chamber below.

HORRIBLE SMELLS WARN US OF ROT AND DECAY AND GERMS. *This tells us not to eat food that has gone bad, or touch items that could make us ill with infection.*

OUR SENSE OF SMELL IS FAIRLY POOR COMPARED TO MANY ANIMALS. *We have about 50 million smell cells, but a dog has 500 million and its sense of smell is probably 1,000 times better than our own.*

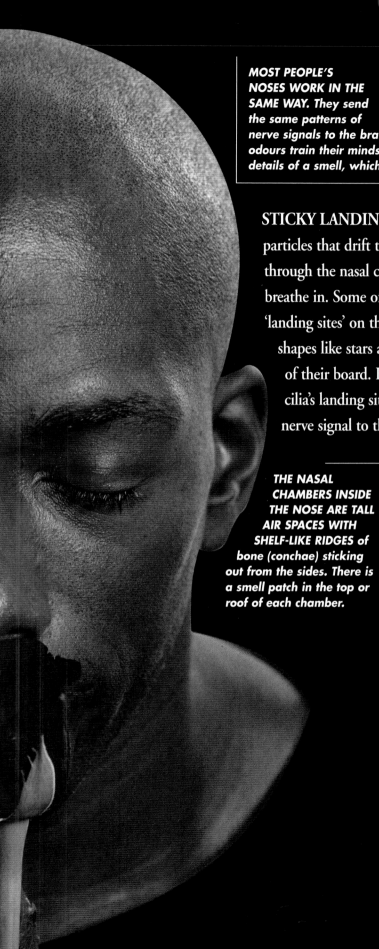

MOST PEOPLE'S NOSES WORK IN THE SAME WAY. They send the same patterns of nerve signals to the brain. But experts on scents and odours train their minds to concentrate on the details of a smell, which other people miss.

STICKY LANDINGS Smells are actually tiny particles that drift through the air. They pass through the nasal chamber whenever we breathe in. Some of these particles fit into 'landing sites' on the cilia, in the way that toy shapes like stars and squares fit into the holes of their board. If a smell particle slots into a cilia's landing site, that smell cell sends a nerve signal to the brain.

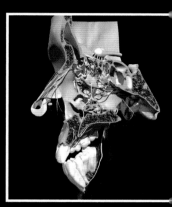

A good sniff makes more air swirl around in the upper nasal chambers, bringing more smell particles to be detected. Just above the smell patches is a bulge, the olfactory bulb (yellow blob), which then extends as the olfactory nerve into the brain.

THE NASAL CHAMBERS INSIDE THE NOSE ARE TALL AIR SPACES WITH SHELF-LIKE RIDGES of bone (conchae) sticking out from the sides. There is a smell patch in the top or roof of each chamber.

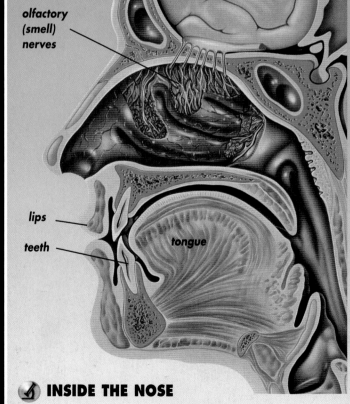

olfactory (smell) nerves

lips

teeth

tongue

🔥 INSIDE THE NOSE

The smell patches are in the upper part of each nasal chamber. Tiny nerve branches gather signals from them and join to the olfactory bulb above. This 'pre-sorts' the nerve signals before they pass into the brain.

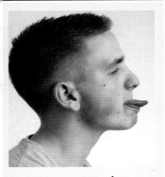
SENSES *Tongue & Taste*

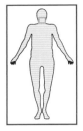

Your tongue is very useful, and not only for tasting food and drink. It can moisten your lips and lick bits of food from them, move food around in your mouth as you chew, change its shape and position as you speak clearly, and even make an appearance outside the mouth which is a sign of rudeness.

A young person has a total of about **10,000 taste buds**.

This number falls by middle age to about 8,000, and **in old age to nearer 5,000**.

This is partly **why older people say that 'foods today have less taste** than when I was young'.

Some people have fewer than 1,000 taste buds while others possess more than 20,000.

PIMPLES *&* BUDS The tongue is made up almost entirely of muscle. It has a thin covering that protects this muscle, covered with small pimple-like bumps and flaps called papillae. These are especially large and lumpy across the back of the tongue. On and around each of these are much smaller sensors called taste buds, each one too small to see. There are many thousands of taste buds at the front, sides and rear of the tongue, but very few in the main middle area.

TONGUES HAVE MANY JOBS, especially keeping the lips, teeth and gums clean. Also, try talking without moving your tongue!

Ouch! It hurts when you bite your tongue or lip. This usually happens because you are thinking of something else, rather than eating. Or perhaps you are trying to talk and chew at the same time. Such damaged areas usually heal in a day or two. However, they may turn into raw, red areas called ulcers, which hurt and sting when you eat. The doctor or pharmacist can advise on treatment.

LIKE SMELL, TASTE IS AN EARLY WARNING SYSTEM for items we might eat and swallow. Some sour and bitter tastes warn us that foods may be rotten or mouldy, and could cause food poisoning.

OUT IN THE WILD, animals trust their instincts and avoid bad-tasting foods. Tongues are also useful for licking skin and fur clean.

IN FOCUS
TASTE BUDS

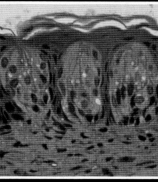

The taste buds are positioned mainly on the sides of the papillae and around their bases, rather than on the flat tongue surface.

THE SIGHT AND SMELL OF FOOD CAUSES A BODILY REACTION, where watery saliva (spit) flows into the mouth. This saliva moistens the food so it is easier to chew. It also releases flavour particles from the food so it is easier to taste.

FLAVOURS GALORE? Our taste buds look a bit like tiny oranges. Each taste bud has taste cells that look like the segments of the fruit. Each taste cell has tiny hairs called cilia at its tip, just like the smell cells found in the nose. Food and drink has different flavours because of different taste particles. Each flavour has a different shape, and if it fits into a 'landing site' on the cilia, then the taste cells send nerve signals to the brain. The vast number of flavours we appreciate are produced by the combination of these tastes with smell. This is why we can't appreciate food properly when we have a cold.

TASTE ZONES

We sense different basic flavours on different parts of the tongue. Sweet flavours are detected mainly at the front tip, salty ones along the front sides, sour along the rear sides, and bitter across the back.

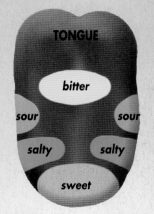

TONGUE

bitter

sour — sour

salty — salty

sweet

THE CHAMELEON LIZARD'S TONGUE IS ALMOST AS LONG AS ITS WHOLE BODY! If your tongue was this length, you could flick it out to grab food which was too far away for your hands to reach.

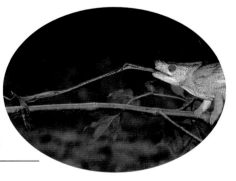

TRY IT YOURSELF

With the dampened end of a drinking straw, put a few sugar grains on the tip of your tongue. Let them dissolve and taste the sweetness. Wash your mouth out and do the same, but put the grains towards the middle rear of your tongue. Can you taste anything?

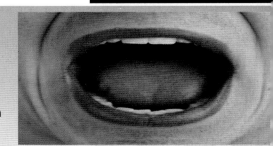

In the sensitive skin of the fingertips there are **50–100 micro-sensors in an area the size of this o**.

In the much less sensitive skin on the small of the back or **outside of the thigh, the same area has just 1–5 microsensors**.

We can **detect temperature differences of only 1–2°C**. For most people about 42–43°C is comfortably warm, while 46–47°C is uncomfortably hot.

SENSES *Skin & Touch*

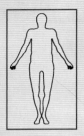

What can you feel right now? You might be touching the pages of this book, but what else? Your clothes and footwear, although perhaps you had forgotten about them. Perhaps you are touching a table or chair too. The body is always in contact with something.

SKIN SENSATIONS Whenever our skin is pressed, microscopic touch sensors just under its surface are stretched and squashed. When this happens, the sensors fire off nerve signals along very thin nerve fibres. The fibres gather together to form thicker nerves which carry the signals from all over the body to the brain. We also feel 'touch' even when something brushes against the hairs yet does not contact the skin. This is because these hairs have nerve endings wrapped around them. These also send signals to the brain as the hairs are moved.

PETS FEEL WARM AND SOFT, which are both pleasing sensations of touch. Stroking them helps us to relax.

The lips are one of the most sensitive parts of the body because they have lots of touch sensors packed together in a small space. This is one of the reasons why babies and young children often put things to their mouths to investigate them - and why adults enjoy kissing!

IN FOCUS
PACINIAN SENSORS

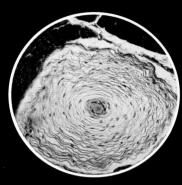

Pressure on the skin is detected by pacinian sensors. These are buried in the deeper skin layer and shaped like tiny squashed onions. They may be more than one millimetre long.

WHY IS TICKLING FUNNY? No one knows. But it works best if the tickler uses a light touch, with a regular brushing motion, and moves gradually across the skin. Surprise is also important – it's very difficult to tickle yourself!

MANY KINDS OF TOUCH FEELINGS Like all of our senses, touch is more complicated than it seems. There are different sizes and shapes of microsensors in the skin, and they respond in different ways, sending complex patterns of nerve signals to the brain. These patterns let us know the type of touch we are receiving. The signals also tell us if the item we are touching is warm or cold, smooth or rough, hard or soft, and still or moving.

WE CAN LEARN COMPLEX MOVEMENTS BY TOUCH ALONE, without having to look, from tying shoelaces to playing music. The brain concentrates on the feelings from the hands and fingers, and moves the muscles in well-practised ways.

TRY IT YOURSELF

We can identify an object and build up a picture of it in the brain, just by touch. Place about eight common items on a table, close your eyes, and pick up one. You probably know what it is straight away by its size, shape and feel, from hard, cool metal to softer wood, smooth plastic or squishy sponginess.

SKIN SENSORS

There are about eight different kinds of microscopic sensors in the skin. The largest are about half a millimetre across, the smallest 100 times tinier.

Breathe in deeply through your nose. What can you smell? Perhaps a scent or deodorant, maybe air-freshener or flowers, even a 'people' odour of clothes and sweat. As you breathe in, oxygen begins a journey through your respiratory system, which could end at your fingers and toes!

NEED FOR OXYGEN The main purpose of the respiratory system is to get oxygen into the body. Oxygen is a gas that makes up about one-fifth of the air. It is needed in the body because it takes part in a process where glucose, a type of sugar, is broken apart to release the energy it contains. This process occurs many times every second, in every microscopic cell of the body. It is called cellular respiration. The energy it releases is then available to power the cell's hundreds of other life processes. It can be confusing, because the action of breathing is also called respiration.

WE CAN BREATHE in through the nose and mouth. The nose is more specialized to take in air, while the mouth is usually seen as part of the digestive system.

IN FOCUS
AIRWAYS AND LUNGS

POISONOUS WASTE Our cells need a continuous supply of oxygen. When they use oxygen, however, cells make a gas called carbon dioxide. This would be poisonous if it built up inside the body. The respiratory system gets rid of the carbon dioxide. Our respiratory system also helps us in other ways. It helps with our sense of smell, and also with the power of speech.

THE INNER LININGS OF THE AIRWAYS and lungs are moist. As air comes out it carries this dampness as water vapour. When the air around is cold, the vapour condenses or turns back into tiny droplets of water – 'cold steam'.

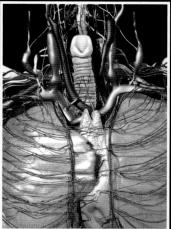

A front view reveals the voice-box at the top of the windpipe, and how high the lungs extend.

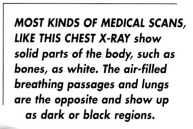

MOST KINDS OF MEDICAL SCANS, LIKE THIS CHEST X-RAY show solid parts of the body, such as bones, as white. The air-filled breathing passages and lungs are the opposite and show up as dark or black regions.

✋ AIRWAYS

The main passage for air in the respiratory system is through the nose, around the rear of the palate to the throat, and down the windpipe to the lungs in the chest.

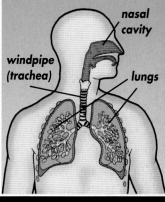

nasal cavity

windpipe (trachea)

lungs

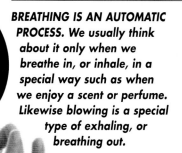

BREATHING IS AN AUTOMATIC PROCESS. We usually think about it only when we breathe in, or inhale, in a special way such as when we enjoy a scent or perfume. Likewise blowing is a special type of exhaling, or breathing out.

✋ TRY IT YOURSELF

How many ways can you breathe out? Often we use out-breaths to show our thoughts and emotions in an unspoken way. You could breathe out softly as a sigh of sadness, or slightly harder when you give up on a problem, or harder still to show irritation.

On average, the inside of the nose makes about **enough mucus every day to fill two egg-cups**.

During normal breathing, air flows in and out of the nose at about **2 metres per second**.

During a cough it rushes out of the mouth **at 20 metres per second**.

During a sneeze it **blasts out of the nose at 30 metres per second**.

Some people have an allergy or sensitivity to tiny floating particles in air, like dust or plant pollen. The lining inside the nose tries to 'fight' these particles as if they were harmful germs. The lining becomes swollen and itchy with runny nose and sneezing. The general name for this condition is allergic rhinitis. Allergy to pollen is sometimes called 'hay fever'.

LUNGS *UPPER AIRWAYS*

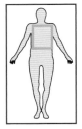

Sniff, sniff, blow ... when you have a cold, or go out in the windy winter sun, or shed a few tears, your nose may drip or run. It needs a good blow into a paper tissue or handkerchief to clear it. A runny nose can be annoying. But the slimy, sticky mucus has a vital job, to protect the delicate lining from drying out and thus preventing attack by germs.

IN FOCUS
UPPER AIRWAYS

INSIDE THE NOSE The nose is the body's air-conditioning unit. It warms, moistens and filters incoming air. The nose's two holes, nostrils, lead into twin air spaces just behind the nasal chambers. Each is bigger than a thumb and has a lining which is damp with mucus and also rich in tiny blood vessels. As the air flows in, it is warmed and moistened, which makes it better prepared to enter the very delicate lungs.

DOWN THE THROAT There are hairs in the nostrils that trap dirt and dust. Also, tiny particles such as germs stick to the mucus-covered lining inside the nasal chambers. So the air is filter-cleaned too, which does not happen if it is breathed in through the mouth. The mucus of the nasal lining is always being made. It usually passes back and down into the throat, perhaps helped by a sniff, and swallowed. If an infection by germs causes extra mucus, we remove this by blowing the nose.

SOME FORMS OF AIR POLLUTION CAN be seen, like smoke and bits of floating powder or dust. But many harmful gases and fumes are unseen. They include the tiny particles from old vehicle engines, especially diesel engines.

tonsils

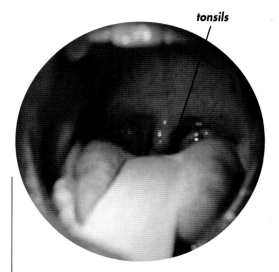

LUMPY PATCHES CALLED TONSILS lie at the back of the throat. As parts of the disease-fighting immune system they may become swollen, red and painful during infection by germs.

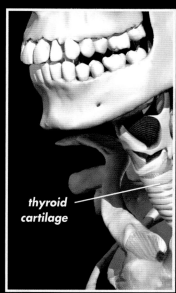

thyroid cartilage

The large, curved thyroid cartilage in the front of the upper neck, with two prongs facing up and down at each side, protects the lower throat, voice-box and windpipe.

SINUSES

Branching out from the nasal chamber are small passageways leading to four pairs of sponge-like, air-filled spaces. These are inside the skull bones around the face, and are called sinuses.

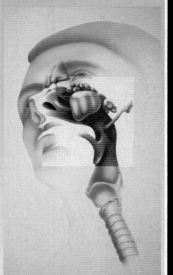

AH-TISH-OOOOOW!
A sneeze blasts air up the throat, through the nasal chambers and out of the nose. It happens when the nose is itchy or blocked, to clear the problem.

TRY IT YOURSELF

Speak normally, then while holding your nose. Your voice sounds very different. As you talk normally, sounds come out through the mouth and nose. The nasal chambers and the sinuses give the voice a fuller, richer sound. Holding your nose stops this.

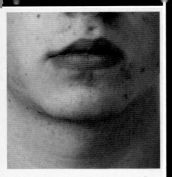

The voicebox is made from ten pieces of cartilage, the largest being the thyroid cartilage which forms the 'Adam's apple'.

There are also about 15 muscles in and around the voicebox, which are involved in speech.

Most men have longer, thicker vocal cords compared to most women, so their voicebox vibrations are slightly lower, making their voices deeper.

If you have had to stay silent for a time – perhaps a 'sponsored silence' to raise money for a good cause – you know how important our voices are. We can send text messages, e-mails and posted letters. But the sounds made by the voicebox are our main means of communication with others.

IN THE NECK The voicebox, or larynx, is between the base of the throat and the upper part of the windpipe, or trachea. Its main structure is made of curved parts of cartilage, or 'gristle', which is similar to bone but slightly softer and more bendy or springy. The largest of these cartilages is called the thyroid cartilage, at the front. It makes a bulge under the skin in the front of the neck known as the 'Adam's apple'.

FOLDS NOT CORDS Two vocal cords are found in the larynx. They look like folds or ridges, one on either side, sticking out into the airway. Normally the vocal cords are apart so we can breathe without making a sound through the gap between them,

IN FOCUS
DOWN TO THE CHEST

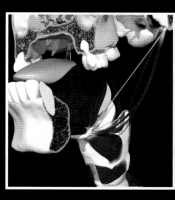

To speak or sing higher notes, the muscles in the voicebox pull the vocal cords and stretch them tighter, so they vibrate faster.

(known as the glottis). To make sounds, muscles pull the vocal cords almost together, leaving just a narrow gap. As air passes up from the lungs and through this gap it makes the vocal cords vibrate. These vibrations make the basic sounds of the voice. Our throat, mouth, nose chamber and sinuses make these noises louder, and the tongue, teeth and lips help us to produce clear speech.

Above the voicebox is the leaf-shaped flap of the epiglottis cartilage. When food is swallowed this folds down over the entrance to the voicebox, to prevent the food entering the airway and causing choking.

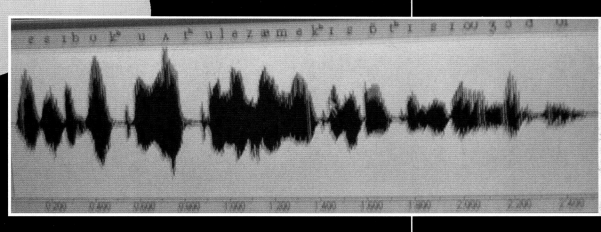

NO TWO PEOPLE HAVE EXACTLY THE SAME SHAPE OF VOICEBOX, throat, nose and mouth. So the sound of each person's voice is unique. A picture of the sound waves is called a sonogram or 'voiceprint'. It can be used like fingerprints to identify people for security reasons.

VOICEBOX

The voicebox is a chamber of complicated shape, made of cartilage, muscles and elastic-like, strap-shaped ligaments. The vocal cords are shaped like ridges.

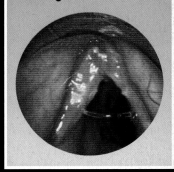

TRY IT YOURSELF

Feel your voicebox while humming, to detect the vibrations there. Make the hum louder and the vibrations become greater. Change your lip positions to make an 'eeee' and then 'oooo' and see how the mouth alters the basic sound of the vocal cords. Now make a hissing sound like a snake, and the voicebox vibrations stop. The hiss is from air passing through a narrow gap between the tongue and roof of the mouth.

In an adult the windpipe has a **total length of 10–11 cm and is 1.5–2 cm wide**.

Its walls are strengthened with **16–20 C-shaped pieces of cartilage**.

The right main bronchus is **2.5 cm long**, and the left one nearer **5 cm in length**.

If all the different-sized air tubes in the lungs could be joined end to end **they would stretch more than 50 km**.

LUNGS *LOWER AIRWAYS*

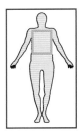

Every time you move your head and neck, you twist and bend your windpipe, or trachea. This is the main airway tube leading down to the chest.

HOLDING THE AIRWAYS OPEN The windpipe must keep itself open against the body's internal pressure. So its walls are strengthened with C-shaped pieces of springy cartilage ('gristle'). These make the windpipe very strong yet flexible and hold it open against the push of the parts around, allowing air to flow freely. At its base the windpipe divides into two slightly smaller tubes known as bronchi. One bronchus leads to each lung. Then the bronchus divides into smaller tubes, which also divide, and so on. All of these tubes have cartilage rings to keep them open too.

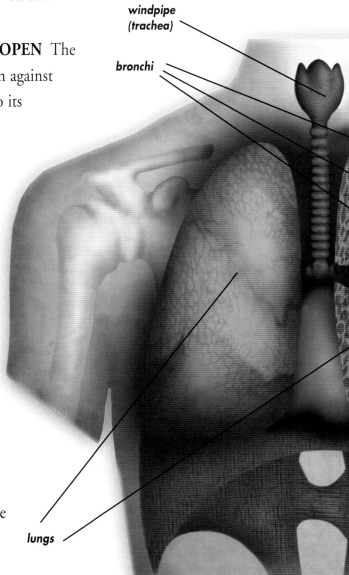

windpipe (trachea)

bronchi

lungs

IN FOCUS
TREE IN THE CHEST

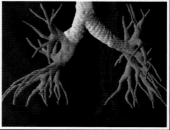

The branching pattern of air tubes in the lungs is known as the bronchial tree. Its narrowest 'twigs' (not shown here) extend into every part of each lung. The whole 'tree' sways and bends like a real one with each breath, as the lungs enlarge and deflate.

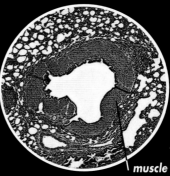

muscle

The walls of all but the smallest airways have a layer of smooth or involuntary muscle. This is designed to contract and narrow the airways automatically, in case of emergency, such as to keep out toxic fumes. But it can also contract due to an allergy such as asthma.

A BRONCHOSCOPE is a telescope-like device for looking down the throat into the windpipe and bronchi. It shows the strengthening pieces of cartilage and checks for blockages, infection by germs and other problems.

KEEPING CLEAN The windpipe, bronchi and bronchioles have a special 'self-clean' lining. Like the inside of the nose, the lining continuously makes a thin layer of sticky mucus to trap dust and germs. The lining is also filled with millions of tiny hairs called cilia, which push the mucus along, up the air tubes and windpipe to the throat, where it is regularly swallowed. This cleaning process keeps the lungs from becoming clogged up with dirt and germs.

HOUSE DUST MITES are tiny creatures which thrive in dust, carpets, curtains and beds. Their droppings dry into a powder that floats easily and, when breathed in, can cause the wheeziness of asthma.

THE WINDPIPE IS DIVIDES INTO TWO LARGE TUBES, which divide again to carry air deep into the lungs.

🔧 BRONCHIOLES

Starting with the windpipe and its division into the main bronchi, another 23 or so divisions result in thousands of tiny air tubes called bronchioles, deep in the lungs. When an asthma sufferer has an asthma attack, these airways contract, making it more difficult to breathe.

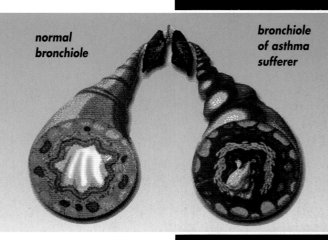

normal bronchiole

bronchiole of asthma sufferer

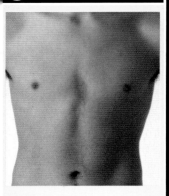
LUNGS *Deep in the Lungs*

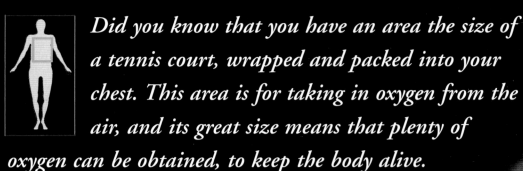

Did you know that you have an area the size of a tennis court, wrapped and packed into your chest. This area is for taking in oxygen from the air, and its great size means that plenty of oxygen can be obtained, to keep the body alive.

In both lungs of an adult there are about **300 million alveoli**.

If they were all flattened out their surface area would be about 50 sq metres when the lungs have breathed out, and up to 150 square metres when they breathe in.

The total area of the capillary blood vessels around all the alveoli is about 100 square metres.

FULL OF BUBBLES By the time the airways in the lungs have branched more than 20 times, they are thinner than hairs and number more than 10 million. Each of these tiny tubes is called a terminal bronchiole. At its end it has a bunch of bubble-shaped air spaces, looking like grapes on their stalk. The air spaces are called alveoli. The alveoli make up about one-half of the total volume of the lungs. The rest is made up from the various branching airways of the bronchi and bronchioles, and also two sets of branching blood vessels. These are the pulmonary arteries bringing low-oxygen blood from the heart, and pulmonary veins taking high-oxygen blood back again.

THE CAPILLARIES Like the airways, the pulmonary arteries divide and become smaller and smaller until they form the body's tiniest blood vessels, capillaries. A net-like set of capillaries surrounds each alveolus. The walls of the alveolus and the capillary are so thin, only 1/500th of one millimetre, that oxygen can easily pass from the air inside the alveolus, into the blood. At the same time the body's waste product carbon dioxide seeps the other way and is removed when the air is breathed out.

IN FOCUS
CHEST CONTENTS

airways

This illustration of the chest with the heart and lungs removed shows the branching airways and blood vessels within the breathing muscles of the rib cage.

IF THE INSIDE OF THE CHEST WAS ONE LARGE HOLLOW SPACE, it would have an area of less than half a square metre – far too small to take in enough oxygen to survive. The alveoli increase the area more than 100 times, to more than the area of a tennis court.

lung cancer

THIS COLOURED X-RAY shows an area of a cancerous growth (tumour) caused from smoking.

ALVEOLI

The main bulk of the lungs is made of millions of tiny bubble-like alveoli. As blood flows through the capillaries around the alveoli, it takes in oxygen and turns bright red.

TRY IT YOURSELF

Hold a dangling paper tissue at arm's length. Aim a gentle blow at it, but with your mouth fairly wide open. See how much the tissue sways in the 'breeze'. Then make the same blowing effort but through a small hole between pursed lips. This forces the air out faster and harder, and the tissue should move more.

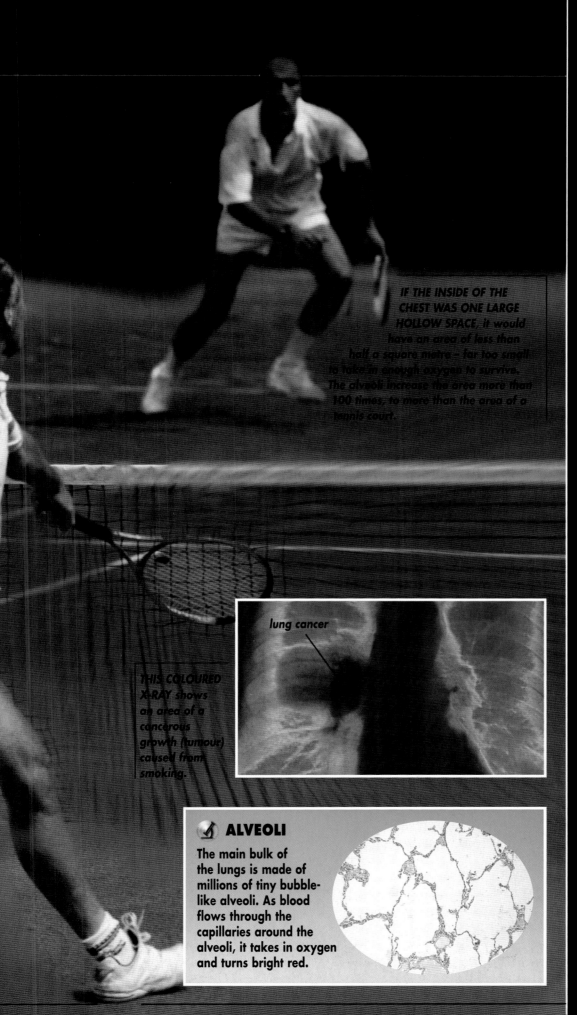

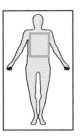

At rest, each breath takes in and then pushes out about **half a litre of air.**

The average breathing rate at rest is **12–15 breaths per minute.**

After great effort, the breathing volume rises to more than 3 litres, and rate to **50 breaths per minute.**

So, the total amount of air breathed at rest each minute **rises from 6–8 litres** at rest, to 150 litres or more after lots of exercise.

HEALTHWATCH

The respiratory system is one of the main ways that germs get into the body. Many are filtered out by nose hairs or trapped by mucus. But some pass through the delicate linings inside the nose, throat or lungs. They cause various infections, like colds and sore throats. Sneezing into a tissue or handkerchief avoids spreading them, otherwise tiny germ-carrying droplets can spray several metres.

LUNGS *Breathing*

Breathing is one of the most basic actions of the human body. We can control it if we want to, like when we speak, swallow, suck a drink up a straw or blow our nose.

IN WITH THE FRESH AIR Like other body movements, breathing is muscle-powered. Normal breathing, at rest, involves two kinds of muscles. One is a curved sheet of muscle under the lungs, called the diaphragm. It is shaped like an upside-down bowl. When it tightens or contracts, it becomes flatter. This pulls down the bases of the lungs and so stretches the lungs bigger, sucking air down the windpipe into them. The other muscles are called intercostals and they are between the ribs. When they contract they make the ribs lift and swing out. This also stretches the lungs and sucks air into them.

OUT WITH THE STALE AIR Breathing in needs muscle effort, but breathing out does not. The lungs are stretched like elastic, and when the diaphragm and intercostal muscles relax, they spring back to their smaller size. This blows out the

LIKE OTHER FISH, LUNGFISH TAKE IN OXYGEN BY FRILLY GILLS under flap-like covers in the neck region. But they can also gulp air into a bag-like part near the stomach, which works like a lung. And they take in oxygen through their damp skin. So they can 'breathe' in three different ways!

BUSY MUSCLES NEED LOTS MORE OXYGEN, brought by the blood. So, the lungs breathe faster and deeper to take in this extra oxygen. Stooping slightly, with arms forward and down, makes deep breathing easier.

THE FASTEST SPEED THAT AIR CAN BE BLOWN OUT OF THE LUNGS is called the peak flow. It is measured by blowing hard into a small tube-shaped device. The reading helps doctors to identify breathing or lung problems like asthma.

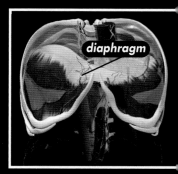

diaphragm

The diaphragm is a large, double-domed, sheet-shaped muscle at the base of the lungs. It forms the boundary between the thorax (chest) above it and the abdomen below. The gullet and major blood vessels pass through it.

stale air which contains less oxygen but more carbon dioxide from the lungs. The lungs are surrounded by two slippery, bag-like layers called the pleurae, which allow them to slide easily inside the chest as they get bigger and smaller with each breath.

TRY IT YOURSELF

Sit quietly for five minutes and then count the number of breaths in one minute. ('In' and 'out' counts as one breath.) Then jog or skip for two minutes, sit down, and count the rate again each minute for the next three minutes. How fast does your breathing rate return to normal? How do your friends compare?

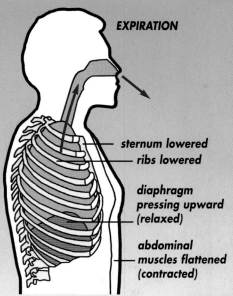

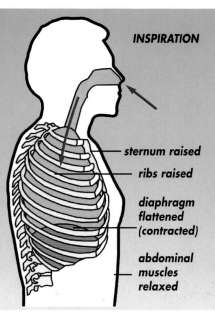

INSPIRATION

EXPIRATION

sternum raised

ribs raised

diaphragm flattened (contracted)

abdominal muscles relaxed

sternum lowered

ribs lowered

diaphragm pressing upward (relaxed)

abdominal muscles flattened (contracted)

FLEXIBLE LUNGS

The muscles of breathing, or respiration, expand the flexible lungs so that more air flows into them. These movements make the chest rise and fall with each breath. As the diaphragm flattens it also pushes the stomach and guts below it, making the belly bulge outwards.

If the body was as big as a large city like London or New York, **its main blood vessels would be like motorways 150 metres across**, and its tiniest vessels would be about the width of a pencil.

The heart, blood and all the blood vessels make up about **one tenth of the weight of the whole body**.

If all the blood vessels in the body could be joined end to end, **they would go around the world more than twice.**

◉ HEALTHWATCH

What we eat, drink and do every day all have huge effects on our heart and blood vessels. Smoking, too much food rich in animals fats, lack of exercise and being overweight cause big problems. They are known as 'risk factors' for heart disease. Each risk factor on its own has a bad effect, and two or more combined make the risk to our health much worse.

HEART ENGINE OF LIFE

Our body has one bag-shaped muscle which we cannot relax, and which must keep working at all costs. This is the heart, the muscle-powered pump for the circulatory system. It beats every second to force blood through the network of blood vessels.

ROUND AND ROUND Our blood goes around and around, or circulates, through the body. It delivers oxygen to all body parts, organs and tissues. Blood also carries hundreds of other substances. These include energy-packed sugars, nutrients for growth, vitamins and minerals to keep the body working well, disease-fighting microscopic white cells, and the 'messenger' substances known as hormones which control many bodily processes.

ALWAYS BUSY Blood not only delivers – it collects too. It gathers up wastes for removal by other body parts. These are the two lungs, which get rid of the waste carbon dioxide, and the two kidneys, which filter unwanted substances from the blood to form the liquid urine. Blood also helps to keep our bodies at a regular temperature. It spreads heat from hard-working parts, like the heart and muscles, to cooler areas. If the body gets too hot, more blood flows through the skin and loses the extra warmth to the atmosphere.

ANY KIND OF MOVEMENT *means muscles work harder, and need extra supplies of oxygen and energy. So the heart pumps harder and faster to increase blood flow through the muscles.*

IN FOCUS
LOCATION OF THE HEART

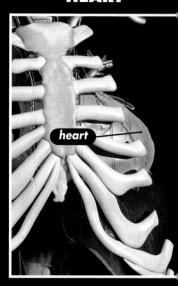

heart

The heart, shown here with its pale grey covering (the pericardium), is behind the breastbone.

THE BODY'S CIRCULATORY SYSTEM works like a giant production line. There are branches into every area, and vehicles come and go as they drop off fresh supplies and gather up wastes.

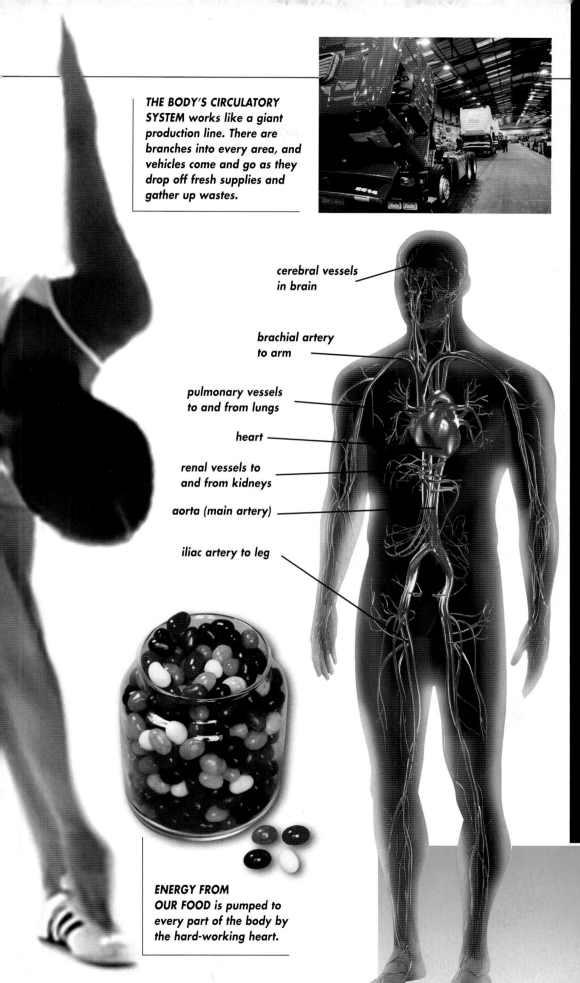

cerebral vessels in brain

brachial artery to arm

pulmonary vessels to and from lungs

heart

renal vessels to and from kidneys

aorta (main artery)

iliac artery to leg

ENERGY FROM OUR FOOD is pumped to every part of the body by the hard-working heart.

✋ TRY IT YOURSELF

In a quiet place, put your fingers into your ears. You may be able to hear the sound of the blood flowing through them, pulsing with each beat of the heart. It makes a very deep thudding sound, like far-off thunder.

🩸 BLOOD VESSELS

The main blood vessels are named after the medical terms for the body parts they supply, such as the renal vessels leading to the kidneys.

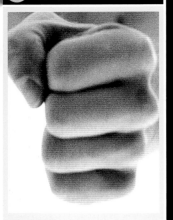
The heart is about **the size of its owner's clenched fist**.

In an average adult male the heart **weighs about 300 grams**, around the same as a medium grapefruit.

In **a typical woman** the heart weighs about 250 grams.

The lower-most pointed tip of **the heart is about level with the sixth rib**.

HEART *The Heart up Close*

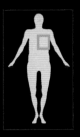

'In love, your heart skips a beat'. The heart is a favourite subject of singers, writers and poets. Sadly their words are not really accurate. Love, courage and kindness come from the brain, not the heart. Yet even the clever brain relies on the heart to survive.

PEAR SHAPED The heart is not really 'heart'-shaped, as in cartoons about love. It is more like a squashed pear lying on its side. The heart is mainly a hollow bag with muscular walls, and inside are four hollow chambers. The two upper chambers, atria, are smaller with thin walls. The two lower chambers, ventricles, are much bigger with thick muscle walls. Each atrium connects to the ventricle below it through a flap-like valve. Blood flows into the heart via the atria and out of the heart via the ventricles.

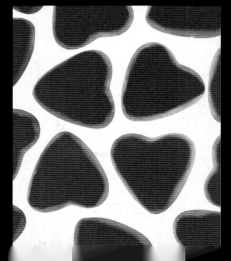

THE TYPICAL CARTOON 'HEART' SHAPE IS A USEFUL SYMBOL, but not accurate. The human heart is shaped more like a squashed pear or pointy-ended potato.

PUMP, PUMP, PUMP, hour after hour, year by year. Mechanical pumps last 10 or even 20 years. The human heart continues for 70, 80, even 100 years.

TWO IN ONE The heart is not a single pump. Rather, it is two pumps side by side. The right pump has one upper atrium and one lower ventricle. Low-oxygen blood comes into the right atrium from all around the body, passes through the valve into the ventricle, and flows from there out to the lungs. High-oxygen blood returning from the lungs enters the left atrium, goes through the valve to the left ventricle, and then flows out all around the body. So the body really has two circulations. The short one to the lungs and back is the pulmonary circulation, the long one all around the body is the systemic circulation.

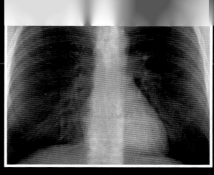

THERE ARE SEVERAL WAYS OF SEEING THE HEART WITHIN THE BODY.
The most common is a chest X-ray. The heart in the X-ray above appears pink. A coronary angiogram outlines the heart's own blood vessels, and an echocardiogram shows its beating motion 'live'.

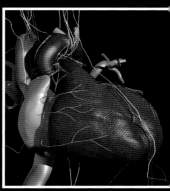

The muscle that makes up the walls of the heart, called cardiac muscle or myocardium, never ceases working and needs a continuing supply of blood.

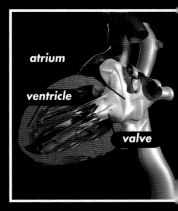

atrium

ventricle

valve

On each side of the heart the small upper chamber, the atrium, receives blood and passes it through a valve to the main lower chamber, the ventricle. This pushes the blood out into the blood vessels.

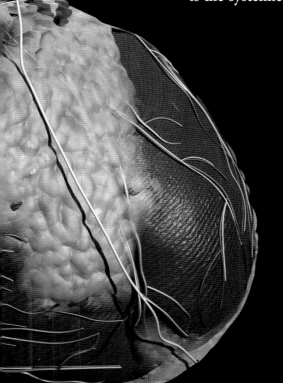

TRY IT YOURSELF

Next time you lie on your back to rest or sleep, look at your chest. You can probably see its breathing movements, but not the heart's motion. However, your abdomen ('tummy') may rise and fall slightly with each heartbeat, as blood pumps into the large vessels inside.

ALMOST ALL KINDS OF ANIMALS HAVE A HEART-LIKE PUMPING ORGAN for body fluids. Usually there is just the one, but the earthworm possesses five in a row along its main blood vessel.

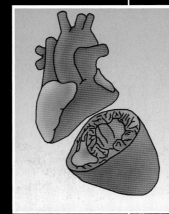

CHAMBERS

A slice through the middle of the heart shows how the smaller right ventricle, sending blood to the lungs, has thinner walls and a curved shape compared to the left ventricle, which pumps blood bodywide.

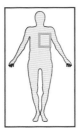

The heart beats almost every second, without you even noticing it. When the body is relaxed, a heartbeat is slow and steady, but when the body is active, the heartbeat gets faster and harder, and you feel it pounding inside your chest.

BLOOD IN Each heartbeat is a smooth, continuous motion. First, the heart muscle relaxes and blood oozes from the main blood vessels into the upper chambers – the atrial. Their thin walls bulge easily. Next, the muscle in each atrial wall gets shorter or contracts. Like a stretched balloon contracting, this squeezes the blood inside the atria and pushes it through the funnel-shaped valve into the ventricle.

IF FRIGHTENED, WE FEEL THE HEART POUNDING FASTER and harder. It is responding to nerve signals from the brain, and also the hormone (message-carrying chemical) adrenaline in the blood.

👁 HEALTHWATCH

You may have heard the expression 'heart murmur'. This is the name that doctor's give to an abnormal sounding heartbeat. By listening to the heart with a stethoscope doctors get used to the sound that a healthy heart makes. Sometimes, though, the heartbeat sounds wrong – there may be a rushing sound, or a click, or a 'whoosh' - and these are called murmurs. Most heart murmurs are due to a problem with the heart valves.

✋ TRY IT YOURSELF

When the body is relaxed, the heart rate is usually 70 beats or less each minute. To find out your pulse, put your first and second fingers on the inside of your wrist and press gently. Count the number of beats every 15 seconds, multiply that number by four and you will have your heart rate in beats per minute.

THE HEARTBEAT IS CAUSED BY TINY ELECTRICAL SIGNALS passing through its muscle. The signals can be detected by sensors on the chest, and shown as a spiky line – the ECG (electrocardiograph).

IN FOCUS
HEART VALVES

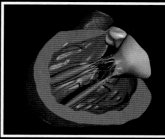

The valves from the upper to lower chambers are called the tricuspid (right side) and bicuspid or mitral (left side). They are made of a tough, leathery material shaped like a funnel, held open by cords.

HEART BEATS

After the atria fill (1), they contract and the valves open (2), to allow blood through to the ventricles. The valves shut when the ventricles contract to stop blood flowing back (3). The valves open as the ventricles contract and blood rushes out into the arteries (4). The sounds of the valves opening and closing make the sound of each heartbeat, 'lub-dup'.

BLOOD OUT

Next, the thicker muscle in the wall of the ventricle contracts, squeezing the blood much harder. This makes the valve into the atrium slap shut, so the blood cannot return there. Instead it flows out through another valve into the main blood vessels – on its way to the lungs from the heart's right side, and around the body from the left side. Then the heart relaxes again, and so the whole process continues.

ONLY RARELY DOES THE HUMAN HEART go as fast as 200 beats each minute. Smaller animals have faster heart rates than us. The tiny shrew's heart, which is smaller than a peanut, beats 1,000 times each minute!

Blood makes up about one twelfth of the weight of the body.

In an average woman, the volume of blood is 4–5 litres.

In a typical man, the volume is 5–6 litres.

At any one moment, only ¹⁄₂₀ **th of the body's blood is in the capillaries**. Most, around three-quarters, is in the veins.

When blood clots in a blood vessel, heart chamber or other site within the body, this is called thrombosis. The clot itself is a thrombus.

HEALTHWATCH
Do you know your blood group? There are two main sets of groups, ABO and rhesus +/- (positive/ negative). They show how blood reacts if mixed with blood from another person. If someone has an accident and needs replacement blood, called a transfusion, the groups must be suited or 'matched'. If not matched, the added blood will clot, clog vessels, and cause serious medical problems— and sometimes even death.

BLOOD *LIQUID FOR LIFE*

Blood is red, thick, sticky, sweet, sealing, healing - and essential for life. It would take many books like this to describe all of the hundreds of substances in blood, and all of the jobs they do.

WHY RED? Blood goes bright red when it contains plenty of oxygen. The oxygen is attached to a substance in blood known as haemoglobin, which gives the red colour. Haemoglobin is found in one of blood's main contents, the tiny red cells. A drop of blood as big as this letter 'o' contains 25 million red cells. They pick up oxygen in the lungs and the blood turns bright red. Then in the capillaries the oxygen passes from the red cells, out to the tissues around. As this happens the colour from bright red to darker reddish purple.

FULL OF GOODNESS Blood contains other kinds of cells too. The main ones are white cells which clean the blood and fight disease. There are also parts of cells called platelets. At a cut or injury, these platelets clump together and the blood goes thicker and sticky. The result is a lump called a clot, which seals the cut and stops more blood leaking away.

In addition blood carries energy in the form of glucose or 'blood sugar', for use by muscles.

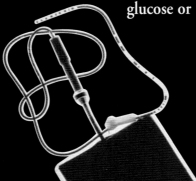

SOME CROPS ARE GROWN HYDROPONICALLY, without soil. The water around their roots contains all the nutrients and minerals they need. Blood is similar, carrying all the substances needed by every body part.

VAST AMOUNTS OF STORED BLOOD ARE USED EVERY DAY by hospitals and medical centres, for people who are ill, injured or having surgery. Giving or donating this blood is very valuable - it can save a life.

IN FOCUS
WOUND HEALING

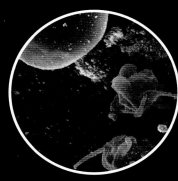

SOMETIMES INJURIES ARE TOO BIG FOR BLOOD TO SEAL BY CLOTTING. They need an emergency covering like a bandage to press on the part, slow down blood loss and keep out germs.

When we suffer a wound, within seconds the damage causes sticky micro-threads of the substance fibrin to appear in the blood. Red cells and platelets get tangled in them and the platelets produce more sticky substances and threads. Eventually a clot forms that plugs the gap.

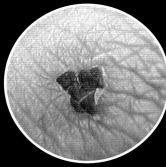

Over a few days the clot hardens into a scab, which protects the area while the damaged parts grow again.

🖐 TRY IT YOURSELF

In a safe place, carefully whirl one arm around like a windmill a few times. Quickly hold both hands together and compare their colours. The force of whirling causes blood to flow down the arm but not back up, so the whirled hand becomes redder.

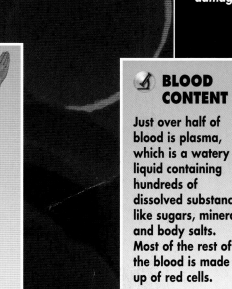

🔬 BLOOD CONTENT

Just over half of blood is plasma, which is a watery liquid containing hundreds of dissolved substances like sugars, minerals and body salts. Most of the rest of the blood is made up of red cells.

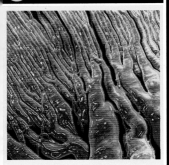

The body's main artery, the aorta, is about 25 mm wide and blood surges through it at 30 cm each second.

A typical smaller **artery is 5 mm wide** and blood flows along at 5 cm per second.

A **capillary is just 1–2 mm long** and only $\frac{1}{25}$ th mm wide.

A large vein is 30 mm wide and its **blood moves very slowly**, less than 1 mm per second.

BLOOD *Blood Vessels*

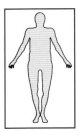

Blood does not slosh around the body like water in a barrel. It flows through a network of tubes called blood vessels. There are three main kinds of vessels – each different in size and structure.

WAVE OF PRESSURE Blood vessels leading from the heart are known as arteries. The largest are about the width of a thumb. Arteries have thick walls, which are very tough and stretchy. Blood comes out of the heart in a surge of pressure, and this makes the artery walls bulge. As this high-pressure surge travels out into the artery network, all of the arteries around the body bulge with it.

TOO SMALL TO SEE As arteries divide they become narrower and their walls get thinner. They lead to all body parts, including the heart itself. Finally they divide into the smallest kinds of vessels, capillaries. The walls of a capillary are so thin that oxygen and other substances can seep through them from the blood inside, to the cells and tissues around. Waste substances move the other way, into the blood.

WIDE AND FLOPPY Capillaries join to make wider vessels, veins. These take the blood back to the heart. By the time the blood has gone through the arteries and capillaries, it has lost most of its pressure. So the vein walls are thin and floppy, and blood flows through them much more slowly.

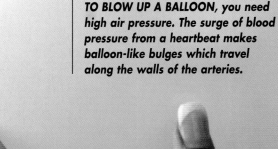

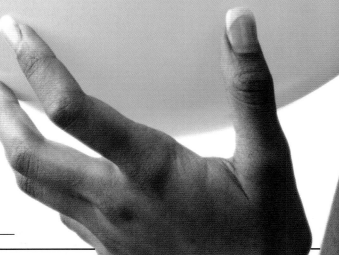

TO BLOW UP A BALLOON, you need high air pressure. The surge of blood pressure from a heartbeat makes balloon-like bulges which travel along the walls of the arteries.

TUNNELS CARRY CARGO AND SUPPLIES QUICKLY PAST AN OBSTRUCTION, like a mountain or river. Arteries do the same, carrying blood swiftly past other body parts until they reach their intended destination.

A CAPILLARY IS SO THIN that even the smallest cells in the body, blood's red cells (see p. 28), have to pass along them in single file.

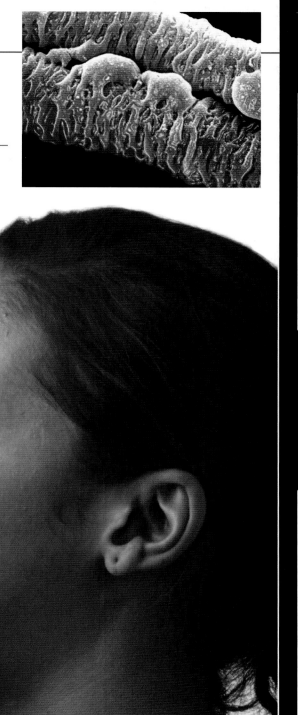

CHEMICAL FACTORIES AND OIL REFINERIES ARE A MAZE OF pipes, tubes, ducts, vessels and channels. But this is nothing compared to the body's network of blood vessels, which would be like a giant factory 50 km long.

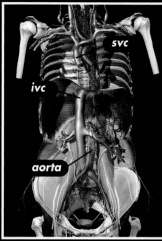

Branches off the central main artery, the aorta, go to the head, arms, abdomen and legs. The main vein returning to the heart from the upper body is the superior vena cava (svc), and from the lower body, inferior vena cava (ivc).

TRY IT YOURSELF

Look at blood vessels, on yourself or an older family member. The veins on the inside of the wrist and forearm are just under the thin skin there. See how the veins come together as they carry blood back up the arm to the heart.

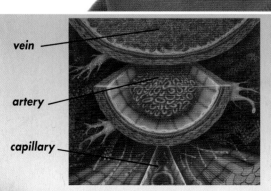

vein
artery
capillary

ARTERIES UP CLOSE

Most of an artery's wall is muscle. Under the brain's control, the muscle can contract to make the artery narrower, and so reduce blood flow to the part it supplies. A capillary is five times thinner than a human hair, and shorter than this 'i'. Its walls are just one cell thick. A vein is wide and flexible, with very thin walls. The main veins have flap-like valves to make sure the low-pressure, slow-flowing blood goes the correct way, back to the heart.

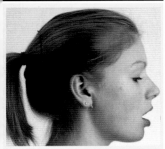

An average adult body contains **around one to two litres of lymph.**

Lymph flows very slowly, less than one millimetre each second.

Lymph nodes range in size from **as small as a rice grain to as large as a big grape.**

The **main groups of lymph nodes** are **in the neck, armpits, groin and inside the lower body**.

During an infection, lymph nodes swell with extra white cells, dead germs and body fluids, to be **larger than tennis balls.**

HEALTHWATCH

Around the world, billions of people are protected from infections by immunisation. Versions of the germs are put into the body. The immune defence system learns to recognise and fight them. Later, if the real germs invade, the defences kill them before they can multiply. This process is called immunisation.

Germs are everywhere - in air, water and soil and on almost every object. But the body fights a silent, never-ending war against them, and lucky for us, usually wins. The invisible armies which defend us against germs and disease make up the immune system.

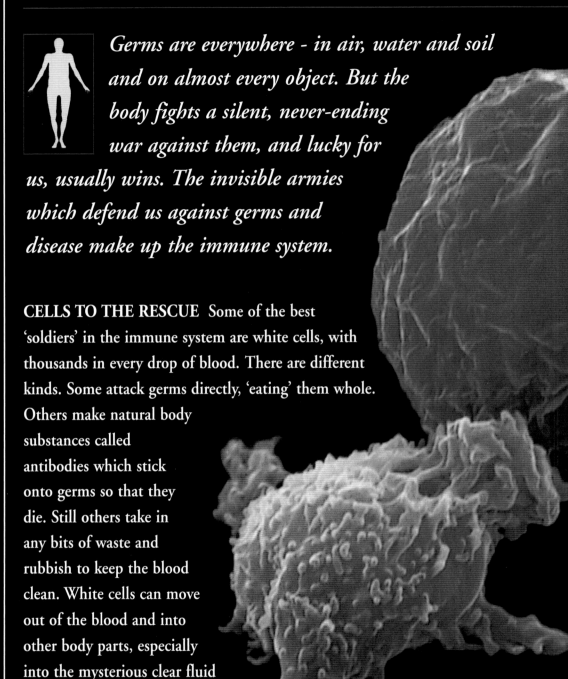

CELLS TO THE RESCUE Some of the best 'soldiers' in the immune system are white cells, with thousands in every drop of blood. There are different kinds. Some attack germs directly, 'eating' them whole. Others make natural body substances called antibodies which stick onto germs so that they die. Still others take in any bits of waste and rubbish to keep the blood clean. White cells can move out of the blood and into other body parts, especially into the mysterious clear fluid called lymph.

PEOPLE ARE CHECKED AS THEY ENTER A COUNTRY, to make sure they are not intending harm. The body's immune system is constantly on guard and carries out similar checks for 'terrorist' germs.

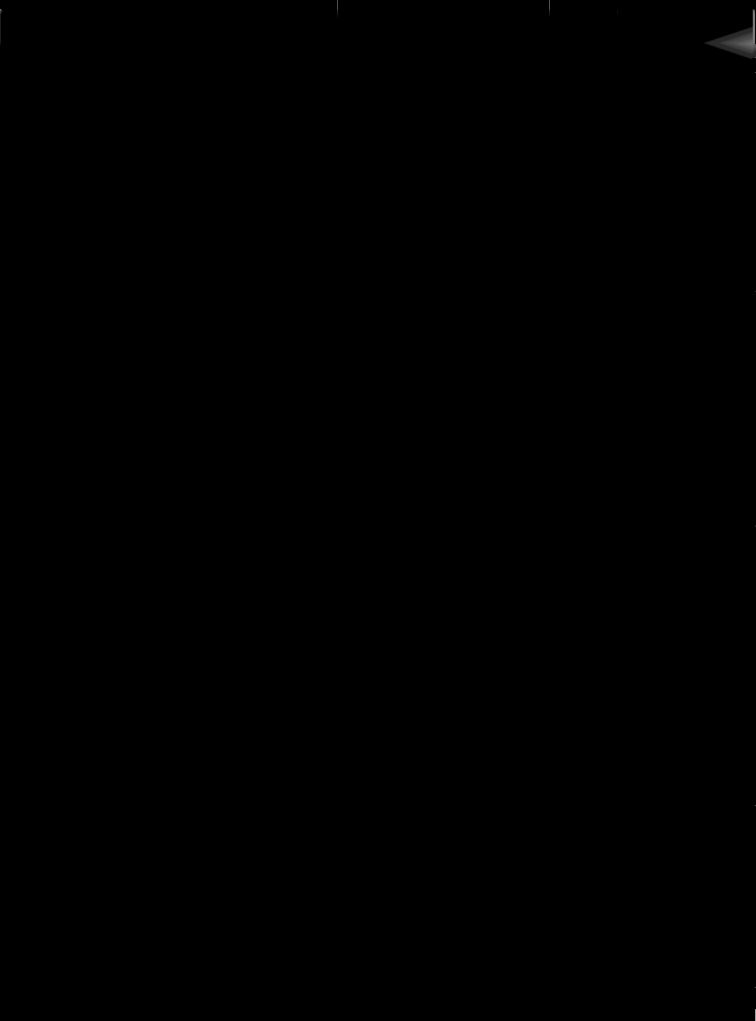

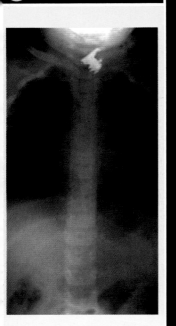
DIGESTION *Digestive System*

The **average length of the adult digestive tract** is about nine metres.

The stomach is about 30 cm around its curve. Food takes between **15 and 48 hours to digest.**

Our bodies need energy to stay active, and even to keep breathing.

GULP! The digestive system has about a dozen major parts which come into action one after the other. Food's first encounter with the body is the mouth. Here the teeth slice and crush it, the tongue tastes it and moves it around for thorough chewing, and the food is moistened with watery saliva from the salivary glands around the jaw. Next the food makes its way down the gullet (or oesophagus) which is a link pipe down through the chest, between the mouth above and the stomach below.

STOMACH &

INTESTINES After a few hours being physically and chemically attacked in the stomach, the mashed food passes to the small intestine, which is very long, and folded and coiled to fit in the abdomen. The small intestine further breaks down or digests the food, and takes the nutrients your body needs into the blood stream.

IN FOCUS
SYSTEM OVERVIEW

Any food left over passes into the large intestine, where water is taken from it according to the body's needs. Finally, the wastes are compacted and stored in the rectum, before being expelled through the anus.

TRACT & SYSTEM The parts above form the digestive tract. But two more organs are vital for the whole digestive system. The pancreas makes powerful juices to aid chemical digestion and the liver receives most of the digestive nutrients from the small intestine. It stores, processes or releases these nutrients.

VAST AREAS OF LAND ARE USED TO GROW OUR FOOD. Farming, harvesting, processing, packing, transporting and selling the stuff that goes into our digestive systems, make up one of the world's largest industries.

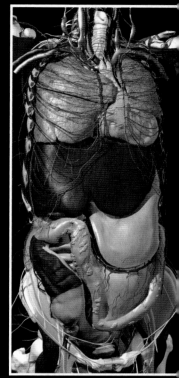

IN A BIOGESTER (ABOVE RIGHT) LEFTOVER FOODS, garden wastes and similar material rot down and release a burnable gas called methane. The body's digestive system also releases burnable gases when it digests food.

Most of the digestive tract is folded and packaged into the abdomen. It almost fills this largest of body cavities, dominated by the dark red liver and paler stomach.

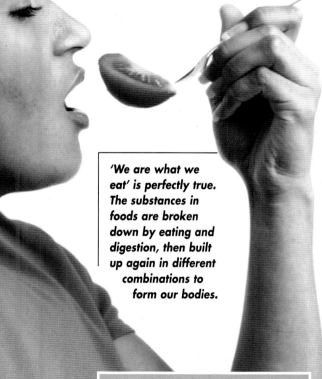

'We are what we eat' is perfectly true. The substances in foods are broken down by eating and digestion, then built up again in different combinations to form our bodies.

👆 TRY IT YOURSELF

At your next meal, slow down slightly. Sit for a time before and after. Chew each mouthful 10 to 20 times. Savour the flavours and enjoy the textures, separately and combined.

🔪 PERISTALSIS AND DIGESTION

Due to pressure inside the body, food must be forced along the digestive tract. It is massaged along or pushed by peristalsis, which is wave-like contractions of the muscles in the tract wall. The process of digestion is carefully timed so that the parts of the tract become active one after the other, as food moves on its journey. This timing is controlled by nerve signals from the brain and 'messenger' chemicals, hormones, in the blood.

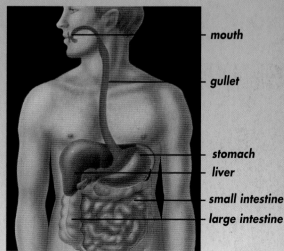

- mouth
- gullet
- stomach
- liver
- small intestine
- large intestine

An average person eats about 500 kg **(half a tonne) of food each year.**

A joule is a measure of energy. Joules in foods are energy in chemical form. **A thousand joules are called kilojoules (kJ).**

The body uses this much energy, in kJ per minute, for:
**Sitting quietly 6-7
Walking 15–20
Running 30-plus**

Foods provide the following energy per gram: **Carbohydrate 16 kJ Protein 17 kJ Fat 35 kJ**

● HEALTHWATCH

Obesity is being overweight – a body which is too heavy for its height. It brings many health problems such as heart disease, clogged blood vessels, breathlessness, strained muscles and joint problems. Various fashionable diets come and go, but the main long-term aims are simple: eat less, exercise more.

DIGESTION *Nutritional Needs*

For good health the body needs a range of different foods. It should not have too much of one food, and not too much of all foods either. Food substances fall into six main groups, and healthy amounts of all are called a balanced diet.

CARBOHYDRATES The body gets its energy from carbohydrates. They are broken down in the body into various sugars, especially glucose, a type of sugar, which is the body's main form of fast energy. Carbohydrates are found in bread, potatoes, parsnips and similar root crops, pastas, rice and other cereals, and various fruits and vegetables.

PROTEINS The body's main building materials are proteins. The protein we get from food is vital to maintain and repair body parts, and for growth in babies and children. Proteins occur in meat and fish, and also in milk, eggs, dairy products and some vegetables, especially peas and beans.

OILS & FATS Body parts like nerves get energy from oils and fats. Too much fat or oil from animal sources, especially fatty meats, can cause problems such as heart disease. Vegetables, fruits and seeds, like sunflower, corn and soya oils provide a much safer form of fats for the body.

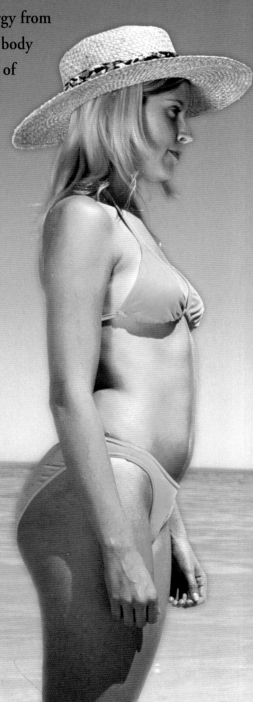

IN FOCUS
ENERGY VS NUTRIENTS

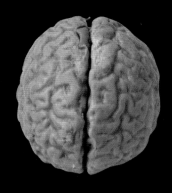

The brain uses far more energy for its size than any other body part. It consumes one-fifth of all energy in food, even though it makes up just one-fiftieth of the body's total weight.

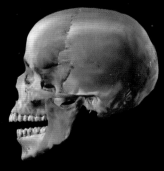

In contrast bones use just one-hundredth of the energy, weight for weight, compared to the brain. But they require from food a far greater proportion of minerals, especially calcium, phosphate and sulphate.

VITAMINS & MINERALS Our bodies need vitamins and minerals in small but regular amounts to avoid illness. Iron, for example, is needed for making red blood cells which carry oxygen in the blood, while calcium helps keep teeth and bones strong, and nerves healthy. Vitamins and minerals are found in most foods, especially fresh fruit and vegetables.

FIBRE Many plant foods contain fibre. Although it is not absorbed by the body, fibre helps the intestines deal with food, and reduces the risk of digestive problems such as certain cancers. Fibre is found in wholegrain products like wholemeal bread, pasta and rice, fresh fruit, leafy vegetables and pulses like beans and lentils.

MORE PEOPLE ARE BECOMING OVERWEIGHT in developed countries. Health experts describe this as an 'epidemic' since obesity raises the risks of many illnesses (see panel).

SOME ANIMALS HAVE A VERY SIMPLE DIET – BLOOD. Mosquitoes, vampire bats, leeches and fleas thrive on this all-round nutritious substance. Our own bodies are designed for a much wider range of foods.

TRY IT YOURSELF

Look at a selection of foods with packaging and see how many joules they contain. Which foods do you think will be the healthiest for you?

🍴 FOOD GROUPS

Simple 'pie' charts colour-code food groups – high-protein meat and fish as yellow, sugar and starch as orange, fresh fruit and vegetables as red, bread and cereal as green and dairy products as blue. This helps to organise a balanced diet.

Look in a mirror, grin widely and poke out your tongue. You will see your digestive 'weapons'. Teeth cut and crush foods, while the tongue keeps food moving to make sure every piece is chewed thoroughly.

TEETH AND SMILES The first set of teeth are the only parts of the body which fall out naturally, to be replaced by a second set. Each tooth has two parts, the crown showing above the gum and the root fixed firmly in the jawbone. Covering the crown is enamel, which is the body's hardest substance. Under this is dentine, which is slightly softer but still very tough. In the root the dentine is 'glued' into the jaw with a layer of cementum. Dentine absorbs knocks and shocks, otherwise chewing would be much more jarring and very noisy. In the centre of the tooth is the pulp of tiny blood vessels and nerves. The sensitive nerves are not just to detect toothache. They also warn of too much pressure when biting, since the whole tooth could crack or snap.

FOOD SCIENTISTS are always testing new flavours to 'tickle our palate', which really means to stimulate the tongue's taste buds.

TEETH CAN GO THROUGH A LIFETIME OF WEAR AND TEAR, *provided they are cleaned daily and checked regularly.*

TASTY TONGUE If you try to eat very dry foods, your mouth soon feels rough and parched. This is because you run out of the watery liquid called saliva or spit. Three pairs of glands make around one and a half litres of saliva each day. On each side of the face the glands are below the ear, in the angle of the jaw and under the tongue. The tongue is almost all muscle – in fact, it's the most bendy muscle in the whole body. It pushes pieces of food between the teeth and holds them for crushing.

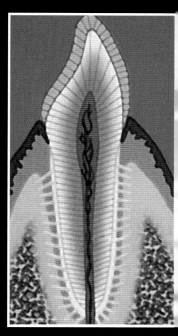

A cutaway canine tooth shows its tall pointed shape, outer enamel with dentine underneath, and delicate dental pulp. As we tear at food we put the canine under sideways stress so it has a root twice as long as its crown.

THE FRONT TEETH HAVE LONG THIN EDGES, *designed to bite and cut mouth-sized chunks from larger food items.*

TONSILS

The mouth is the way into the body not only for food and air, but also for germs. Two lumpy masses on either side of the lower tongue, the tonsils, are part of the body's immune defence system. They become swollen in tonsillitis.

tonsils

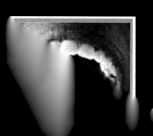

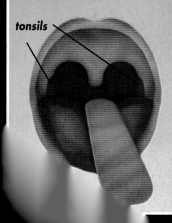

The stomach can enlarge to hold almost two litres of food.

The lining makes about **1.5 litres of gastric juices daily**.

This **lining also replaces itself compeletely** every three days.

There is an old saying: **'Your stomach shrinks if you eat smaller meals**, so you feel full with less food'. But unfortunately this is not true.

HEALTHWATCH

Eating too fast, especially when moving about or talking, can cause several problems. One is gulping down air with the food, which then has to come back – as a belch (burp). Another problem is heartburn. This is caused when too much stomach acid is sent up into the oesophagus, leading to a burning discomfort.

DIGESTION *Stomach*

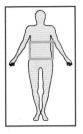

The stomach is virtually in the centre of our bodies. It is very strong and muscular, and can stretch to hold a large meal. While food is in the stomach, it is mashed up and mixed with strong chemicals. By the time food leaves the stomach it is in the form of a thick liquid.

DOWN THE GULLET To swallow food, the back of the tongue pushes a lump of it into the top of the throat. Here the throat muscles 'grab' it and force it over a flap called the epiglottis. This folds down to prevent choking by stopping the food going into the windpipe. The muscles in the throat and then the gullet wall continue to push the food down through the neck and chest, by peristalsis. It takes just a few seconds for the food to reach the stomach.

THE STOMACH IS ON THE LEFT SIDE, with its centre about halfway between nipple and navel. As it expands with a meal its lower end can extend almost to the navel.

The stomach's hydrochloric acid is so strong that if it was made in a factory and put into bottles, it would need a warning label!

POISON

SQUEEZE AND SQUIRM The stomach is not just a stretchy bag that holds food before it passes to the next part of the digestive system. As it fills with a meal, the powerful layers of muscles in the stomach walls make it churn and squirm to squash the chewed food into a pulp. Also, the stomach's lining releases a watery liquid called gastric juice. This attacks the food with powerful chemicals called acids and enzymes. The 'acid bath' of hydrochloric acid in the stomach also helps to kill germs that came in with the food.

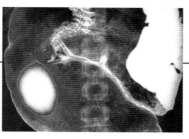

Barium is a substance that shows up as pale or white on X-rays. A barium meal fills the inside of the stomach and shows its shape and position, to reveal problems like tightness or constriction.

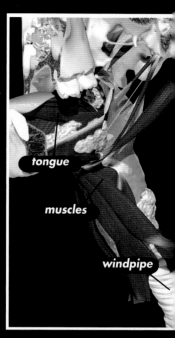

tongue

muscles

windpipe

The base of the tongue extends down into the neck and helps to push food into the gullet, which is behind the windpipe. The strap-like muscles around the upper windpipe and voicebox also help in swallowing.

👆 TRY IT YOURSELF

Ask friends to point to where they think a stomach-ache would be. They may indicate around the navel (belly button). But you know better! The stomach is much higher, just behind the lower left ribs.

🔍 STOMACH WALL

The stomach lining has named regions and is wrinkled and folded (right). Around it are three layers of muscles, each with fibres arranged in different directions.

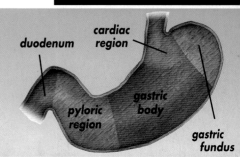

duodenum

cardiac region

gastric body

pyloric region

gastric fundus

The small intestine makes about **1.5 litres of digestive juices each day**.

Foods pass through the small intestine **for up to six hours**.

The lining has a total area which is **almost twice the skin area of the whole body**.

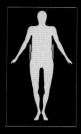

'Guts' can be any parts inside the body, especially digestive parts. But usually 'guts' mean the intestine and perhaps the stomach too. There is one small intestine and one large one.

NUTRIENTS INTO THE BODY On average, if a small intestine was straightened out, it would be seven times longer than the body it came from. The large intestine would be about the same length as the body's height. Mashed, pulped food from the stomach passes in small, regular 'squirts' through a muscular ring, the pyloric sphincter, into the small intestine. This has a lining which is covered with thousands of tiny finger-like parts, villi, each about one millimetre tall. The lining makes more enzymes and other chemicals to finish digesting the food. It also soaks up or absorbs the resulting nutrients, through the villi into the blood stream.

NEAR THE END The small intestine (small bowel) leads to the larger one, which is twice as wide.

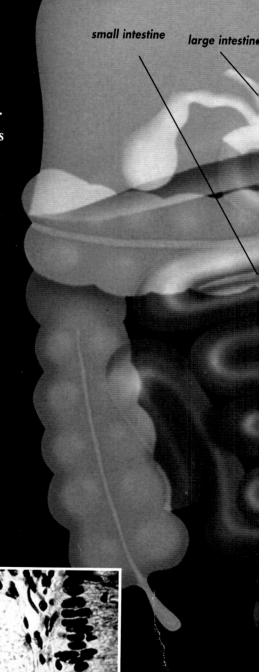

stomach

small intestine

large intestine

INSIDE A VILLUS ARE TINY TUBES OR VESSELS. *Some carry blood, which soaks up the nutrients from the digested food and carries them away around the body. The central tube is filled with lymph fluid, which also takes up nutrients.*

IN FOCUS
GUTS LARGE & SMALL

OOOOOH, THE PAIN OF GUT-ACHE! *This is sometimes due to eating too fast, when food is not chewed properly. Or it could be an infection from germs in food, or a blockage. An X-ray might show the intestines and whether they are swollen, or if food is piling up behind a blockage.*

At the junction there is a finger-size part, the appendix. This is hollow inside but has a closed end and does not lead anywhere. Hard bits of food or germs sometimes get stuck in it and make it swell up, known as appendicitis. In the large intestine, water and minerals are taken from the leftover foods into the blood flowing through its lining. The leftovers become squishy, smelly, brown lumps or faeces. They are stored in the last part of the tract, the rectum, before removal through another ring of muscle, the anus, which also has several other names...

THE LARGE INTESTINE (LARGE BOWEL OR COLON) *forms a 'picture frame' around the small one.*

anus

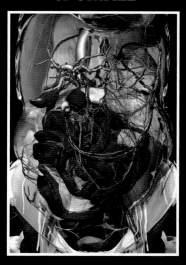

With the liver, stomach and large intestine out of the way, the small intestine is seen coiling its way around the lower half of the abdomen.

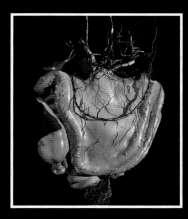

The guts are covered by a large sheet of fatty tissue, the omentum, which drapes like a curtain down the front of the abdomen.

INTESTINAL VILLI

Like the stomach, the small intestine wall has several layers of muscle which make it squirm to push digested food along. The villi form a velvet-like surface inside, almost like a short-haired carpet.

The liver is the body's **largest internal part, or organ**, with a weight of 1.5 kg.

The liver **makes almost one litre of bile daily**. It digests fat in a similar way to how detergents clean our washing up.

The liver contains more blood, in proportion to its size, than almost any other body part.

HEALTHWATCH

A yellow tinge to the skin and eyes is known as jaundice – and is often a sign of liver trouble. Usually the liver breaks down old red blood cells and gets rid of their colouring substance, or pigment, in bile fluid. If something goes wrong the colouring substance builds up in blood and skin and produces jaundice. Infection of the liver by various germs, in different types of hepatitis, can cause jaundice.

DIGESTION *Liver & Pancreas*

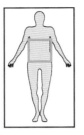

Some machines and people can 'multi-task' and do many jobs at once. Apart from the brain, the liver is the body's best multi-tasker. It has more than 500 jobs, mainly to do with body chemistry.

HUNDREDS OF JOBS The liver has two blood supplies. As well as the normal flow direct from the heart, there is another supply from the intestines, rich in nutrients. What the liver does with these nutrients depends on the body's needs. If blood-sugar levels are already high, the liver may change some of the glucose from digestion into starch. It then stores this starch, known as glycogen, for later times when energy supplies are low. The same storage-or-release happens with many other substances, including vitamins.

The toxins (poisons) which the liver makes harmless include drugs such as alcohol. But too much alcohol overloads the liver and causes the very serious disease known as cirrhosis.

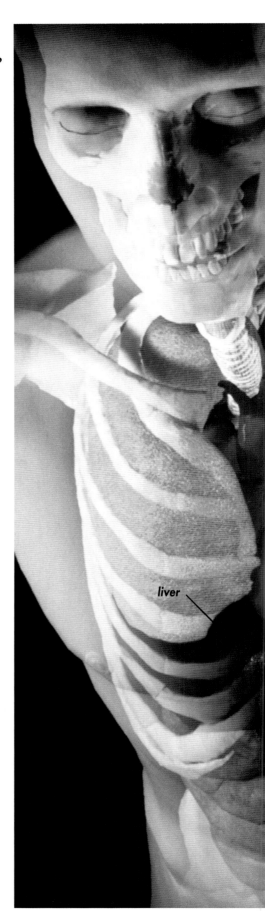

liver

One of the liver's most important tasks is 'detox'. This is detoxification, breaking apart toxins or poisonous substances. The liver also makes a liquid, bile, which is stored in a small bag beneath it, the gall bladder. After a meal, bile flows along the bile duct into the small intestine, where it helps to digest fatty foods.

TWO JOBS In contrast to the liver, the pancreas has only two main tasks. One is to make strong digestive juices containing enzymes. After a meal, these ooze along the pancreatic ducts into the small intestine, where they aid digestion. The pancreas's other main task is to produce hormones.

stomach

The wedge-shaped liver extends at its right side from the level of the nipple almost down to the waist. In this position it is partly protected by the lower right ribs. The pancreas lies just below the stomach, hidden away.

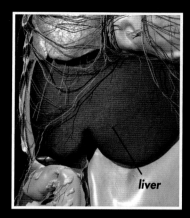

liver

The liver is pressed up against the base of the chest, with most of its bulk on the body's right side. It is dark red in colour due to its massive blood content.

pancreas

With the liver and stomach out of the way, the pancreas is seen lying across the abdomen, over the two kidneys. It is soft and grey-pink, with ducts leading from its blunt right end or 'head' into the small intestine.

✋ TRY IT YOURSELF

If you know any babies or toddlers, take a look at their bulging tummies. It is not the stomach which causes this natural bulge – it is the liver. Compared to an adult, a baby's liver is much larger in proportion to the rest of the body. It takes up almost half the entire abdomen, but only one-quarter in a grown-up.

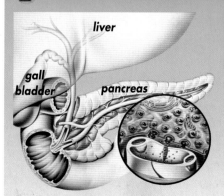

🔍 INSIDE THE PANCREAS AND LIVER

liver

gall bladder

pancreas

Within the pancreas (left) are tiny bunches of cells that make digestive juices. There are also cells which make hormones. The liver (right) has thousands of six-sided, blob-like units called lobules, each about one millimetre across. A lobule has its own blood vessels and also tubes for bile (shown in green) which goes to the gall bladder.

liver lobule

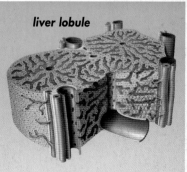

DIGESTION *GETTING RID OF WASTE*

On a hot day when rushing about, you may not need the toilet for hours. On a cold day with little action, you may need it ten times. This difference is due to the way the body balances its inputs of foods and drinks, and its outputs of various wastes - especially the liquid waste we call urine.

FILTERING THE BLOOD The body gets rid of wastes in gas, solid and liquid forms. A waste gas called carbon dioxide leaves from the lungs every time we breathe out. Waste solids leave once or twice daily, as faeces, while the waste liquid urine leaves a number of times. Urine is made by the the kidneys, which are two organs in the back of the upper abdomen. For its size, each kidney has a massive blood flow. Inside the kidney are about one million micro-filters known as nephrons. They remove unwanted substances from blood along with water which the body does not need, as urine.

SOME ANIMALS USE THEIR WASTES TO MARK THEIR TERRITORIES, leaving piles of dung and spraying urine.

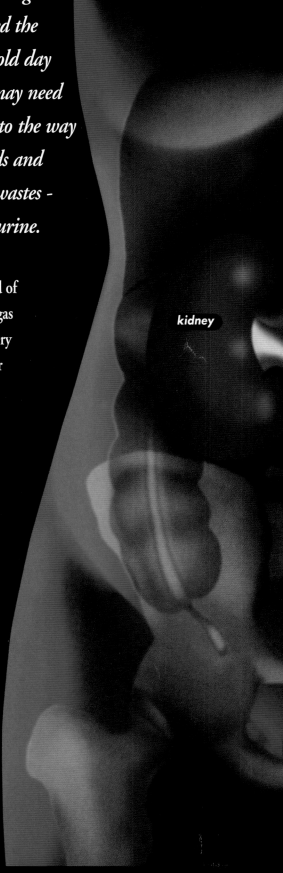

kidney

IN FOCUS
KIDNEYS AND BLADDER

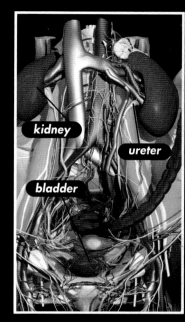

kidney

ureter

bladder

The kidneys' huge blood supply is shown by the size of the renal arteries (red) and veins (blue). The pale ureter tubes lead down to the bladder.

THE KIDNEYS ARE QUITE HIGH IN THE ABDOMEN, *against its back wall, shielded by the lower ribs. The left one is usually slightly higher than the right. The bladder is in the front base of the abdomen. In this picture the kidneys have been brought to the front of the body so you can see clearly where they are.*

ureter

kidney

bladder

urethra

DRIP, DRIP Urine is made by each kidney and collects in its central area, the renal pelvis. It flows down a tube, the 25-centimetre ureter, to the storage bag of the bladder. The bladder gradually stretches and fills with urine until its owner feels the urge to empty it. This is known as urination. A ring of muscle, the urethral sphincter, opens and lets the urine flow along another tube, the urethra, to the outside. The amount of urine made each day varies hugely with how much we eat and drink, how active we are, the temperature, whether we sweat and many other conditions. On average it is about 1,200–1,600 millilitres.

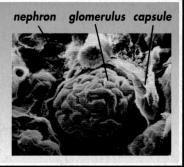

TRY IT YOURSELF

Next time you are active on a hot day, add up how much fluid you drink. Is it more than the usual two or so litres? Most of this extra water is lost as sweat. Drinking lots on a cooler day means more water leaves the body in urine, making its colour paler than normal.

KIDNEY MICRO-FILTERS

Each tiny nephron has a ball-shaped knot of capillary blood vessels, the glomerulus. This is surrounded by a cup-shaped capsule which extends into a long, looped tube. Wastes, minerals and water pass from the blood into the tube. Here useful minerals and some water are taken back into the blood, leaving urine.

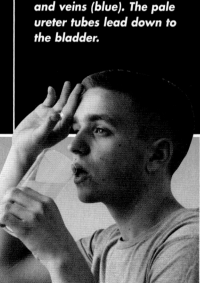

nephron   glomerulus   capsule

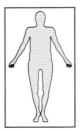

There are many examples of hormones:

Insulin is made by the pancreas, which lies beneath the stomach. It controls the **way our bodies use the sugar, glucose.**

Adrenaline is the hormone which is **released when we become frightened or stressed.** It is named after the adrenal gland, from which it comes.

Thyroxine is an important hormone which **affects just about every part of the body.** It tells the tissues how fast to work.

👁 **HEALTHWATCH**

Several hormones need regular supplies of certain minerals in food. One is iodine, for the thyroid to make thyroxine. In many regions tiny amounts of iodine are added to table salt and cooking salt, and a healthy diet contains enough in any case. But if iodine is severely lacking in food, the thyroid become larger as it tries to make enough thyroxine. The result is a swelling in the neck called a goitre.

DIGESTION *IN CONTROL*

As well as being controlled by the brain through the nervous system, the tissues of your body get instructions from special chemicals in the blood called hormones. These hormones, and the glands which produce them, make up the endocrine system.

TWO SYSTEMS The body has two control systems. The brain and nerves send nerve signals around the body to control its muscles, heartbeat, breathing and many other rapid-action processes. The other control system takes longer to react but also lasts longer. This is the endocrine or hormonal system, using natural chemicals called hormones, made in parts known as endocrine glands. Hormones are released into the blood and travel around the body to affect certain parts, known as targets, usually making them work faster or slower.

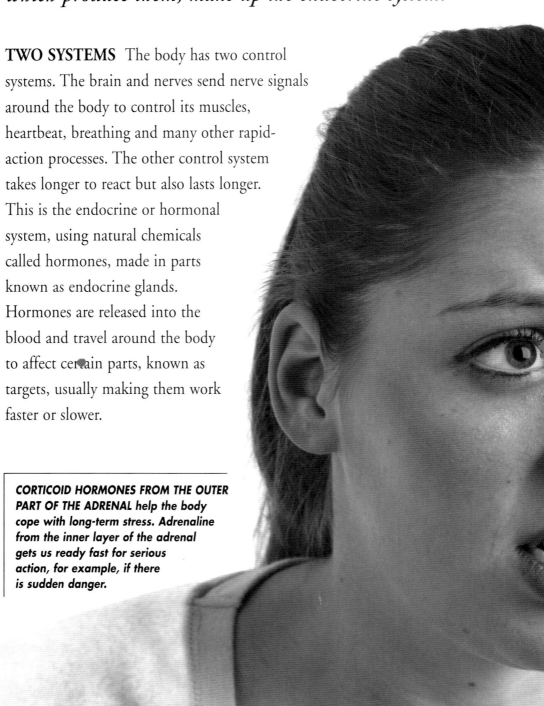

CORTICOID HORMONES FROM THE OUTER PART OF THE ADRENAL help the body cope with long-term stress. Adrenaline from the inner layer of the adrenal gets us ready fast for serious action, for example, if there is sudden danger.

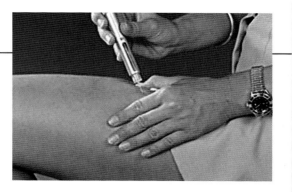

IN FOCUS
HORMONAL GLANDS

IN THE CONDITION KNOWN AS 'DIABETES' THERE IS A PROBLEM MAKING THE HORMONE INSULIN. People with diabetes may have to inject insulin into their bodies every day of their lives.

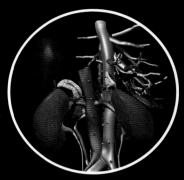

The adrenal glands are shown here as lumpy, pale, curved triangles, seen from the body's rear. They are also called the supra-renal glands, because there is one on top of each kidney.

SMALL BUT IMPORTANT There are more than 100 hormones. About ten come from the pea-sized pituitary, just under the front of the brain. These include the growth hormone, which regulates the body's long-term development, and several hormones that control other hormone-making glands like the thyroid and adrenals. Thyroxine hormone from the thyroid controls the body's rate of energy use and general 'speed' of inner processes.

The thyroid gland wraps around the front of the upper windpipe, just below the voicebox. It is pale and almost X-shaped, its wide left and right lobes joined by a narrower middle section.

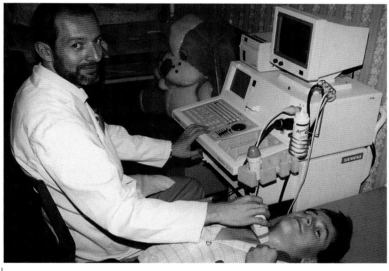

The thyroid is in the front of the neck. Its main hormone, thyroxine, contains the mineral iodine (see Healthwatch). This patient is having his thyroid examined by a doctor.

TRY IT YOURSELF

Next time you are suddenly startled or surprised, check your pulse. The hormone adrenaline will be at work, making your heart beat faster as more blood flows to your muscles, ready for action. Less blood goes to your stomach and intestines, causing 'butterflies in the tummy'.

SEX HORMONES

Males and females produce different hormones which make their bodies change during puberty. Testosterone is the male hormone and is made by the testes. In females oestrogen and progesterone are produced by the ovaries. These hormones are all necessary for reproduction.

In females, **each ovary is 3 cm long** and 1.5 cm wide— hardly the size of a thumb.

In an woman's **average lifetime about 400–500 egg cells are released** in total, from a store of 200,000 in each ovary.

In a male, each testis is about 5 cm long and 2.5 cm wide, and **makes many thousands of sperm cells every second.**

The production of eggs or sperm can be affected in many ways, including unhealthy diet, lack of sleep, worry and stress, and drugs such as alcohol. If eggs do not ripen in a woman, or sperm numbers are low in a man, then a couple who wish to have a baby may have problems. This is known as low fertility. Often, advice from the doctor, and perhaps some simple treatment, can solve the problem.

REPRODUCTION *BABIES*

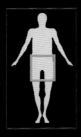

Waaaaaah! Babies can be very noisy and tiring to look after. But we need them to carry on humankind. Reproduction is making more of your kind. A body is either female or male depending on which reproductive parts it has.

FEMALE & EGGS The ovaries are in either side of the lower abdomen. Each month or so, one of them produces a tiny, ripe egg cell. Over several days this egg makes its way along a tube, the oviduct (Fallopian tube), towards the womb. If nothing happens to it then it passes out of the body, along with the blood-rich lining of the womb, through the vagina (birth canal), as the menstrual flow or period. The whole process, the menstrual cycle, then begins again, under the control of several hormones. But if the egg cell meets a sperm cell, the two get together to begin the reproductive process.

From the beginning, each human body is unique with a developing personality, wishes and wants. Even identical twins, who are 'clones' with the same genetic material, become different individuals.

IN FOCUS
OVARIES & SPERM

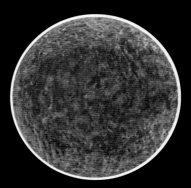

In the ovary, an egg grows and becomes ripe inside a small fluid bag, the follicle. About halfway through the cycle the follicle breaks open and the egg is released, or ovulated, into the oviduct.

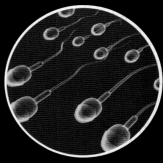

In the testes, sperm begin as blob-shaped spermatocytes, around the inner edge of each seminiferous tubule. Over ten weeks they grow tails and become ripe or mature sperm, in the middle of the tubule.

REPRODUCTION IS A BASIC PROCESS *that occurs in all living things, plants and animals. In humans it also involves feelings of affection, friendship, love and desire–which can become very complicated!*

MALE & SPERM Tadpole-shaped sperm are produced all the time in long tubes known as seminiferous tubules. These are coiled in the two testes, which hang below the front abdomen in a skin bag, the scrotum. The sperm are stored in another long tube, the epididymis, next to each testis. During sex they leave the body in a fluid which passes along another tube, the vas deferens, and then through a gland, the prostate, and along yet another tube, the urethra, which runs through the penis to the outside.

🖊 REPRODUCTIVE SYSTEMS

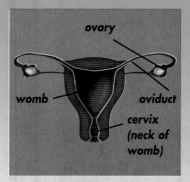

ovary
womb
oviduct
cervix (neck of womb)

THE OVARIES are slightly above and behind the womb. They are held in position in the lower abdomen by strap-like ligaments. The oviducts curl around and down, and lead to the womb, or uterus. This is shaped like a forward-tilted pear.

THE TESTES are below the abdomen, and so slightly cooler than the main body. Sperm production is affected by temperature – too warm and fewer sperm are formed. This would happen if the testes were like the ovaries, within the abdomen.

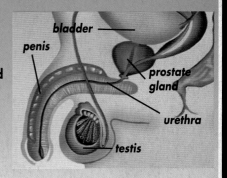

bladder
penis
prostate gland
urethra
testis

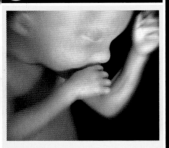
REPRODUCTION *The Body Begins*

There are more than 6,000 million bodies in the world, and they all began in the same way. A tiny egg cell and an even tinier sperm cell came together and joined. The same process is happening now, more than three times each second, to make babies that will be born in nine months' time.

Three weeks after fertilisation the tiny heart is pulsing. Length is 2.5 mm.

After four weeks the eyes, arms and legs start to grow. Length is 5 mm.

After five weeks the brain enlarges greatly and the nose, mouth and intestines are growing. Length is 8 mm.

After six weeks the ears and eyes begin to take shape, the arms lengthen and there is still a tail. Length is 12 mm.

IN THE TUBE As a just-released egg cell drifts slowly along the oviduct of the female system, it may suddenly meet thousands of sperm cells coming the other way. They have completed a very long journey out of the man's body, into the woman's and through the womb. Only one of the sperm joins, or fertilises, the egg. This brings together the genetic material from mother and father, which contains all the instructions needed for a new human body to grow and develop. The fertilised egg cell continues to drift along but within a day it splits or divides into two cells, then four, eight and so on. This is the early embryo stage.

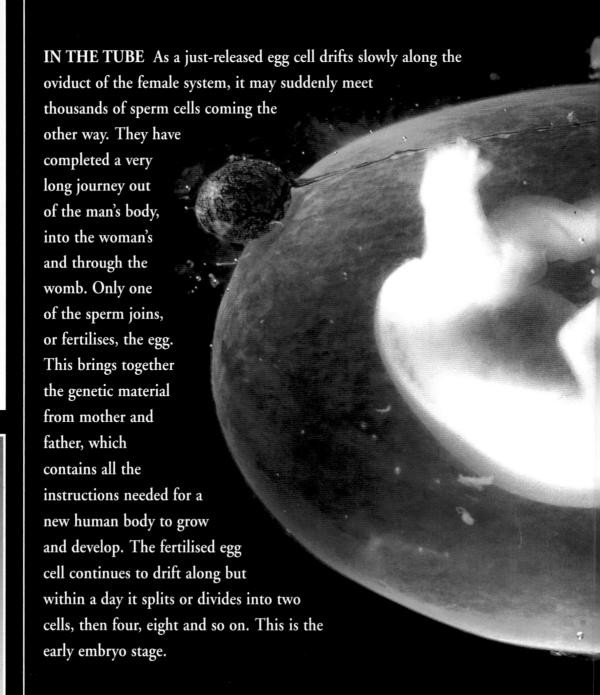

HEALTHWATCH

The mother's health is very important to the growing embryo. It can be harmed if she smokes tobacco, drinks too much alcohol, or takes certain drugs, or lacks nutrients in her food. Even some medical drugs should not be taken during pregnancy. Certain diseases in the mother also affect the embryo's development, such as rubella (german measles).

IN FOCUS
EMBRYO GROWTH

IN THE WOMB About a week after fertilisation the tiny early embryo, as small as the dot on this i, settles into the lining of the womb. The lining has become rich in blood and nutrients as part of the menstrual cycle. The cells of the embryo continue to divide, move about and change shape as they evolve into the cells of body parts like nerves, brain, muscles, and blood. Eight weeks after fertilisation the embryo has become a miniature human body, hardly bigger than a grape, with all its main body parts formed.

Immediately after fertilisation a human egg shows no signs of developing into an embryo.

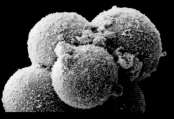

After 2-3 days the embryo's cells start to divide.

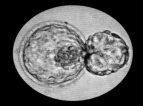

After around six days, the embryo 'hatches' out just before implanting in the wall of the uterus.

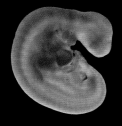

After it has attached to the uterus, the embryo continues to grow, taking on a more recognisable form. This embryo is about four weeks old.

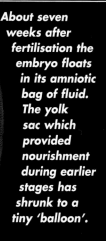

About seven weeks after fertilisation the embryo floats in its amniotic bag of fluid. The yolk sac which provided nourishment during earlier stages has shrunk to a tiny 'balloon'.

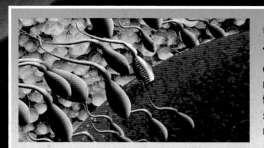

🔬 SPERM MEETS EGG

The sperm is tiny compared to the egg. Its genetic material is in the rounded head end which burrows through the outer layer of the egg, so the male and female genetic material can come together.

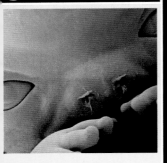
After **four months the baby's bones begin to harden** and the teeth start to grow as tiny 'buds' under the gums. Girls can be told apart from boys.

After **six months the stomach and intestines are fully formed**, the nostrils open and the baby may suck its thumb.

After **eight months fat collects under the skin** but overall growth starts to slow down. The baby has a good chance of survival if born.

Antenatal check-ups are very important for the expectant mother. She receives an examination and also tests such as heart rate and blood pressure. Sometimes problems of pregnancy do not cause obvious symptoms until well advanced. The medical check helps to detect them early, so treatment can be started straight away.

REPRODUCTION *TOWARDS BIRTH*

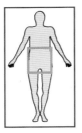

From eight weeks after it began, until the time of birth, the developing baby is known as a fetus. Most of this time is spent growing larger and adding finishing details to the body, like hair and nails.

GROWTH IN THE WOMB In the womb, the baby grows in length by more than 10 times in seven months. It floats in liquid called amniotic fluid inside the womb. At first it can wave its arms and kick its legs, and even turn somersaults. But later the fetus becomes cramped and can move less. In the middle of pregnancy the baby is slim and wrinkled. Towards the end it puts on fat under the skin so it looks more chubby.

THE GREAT DAY After nine months the baby is ready to be born. The muscles in the wall of the womb tighten during contractions and gradually push the baby out, through the cervix (opening or neck of the womb). The baby then passes along the vagina or birth canal, to the outside. Birth can take many hours and is hugely tiring for both mother and baby.

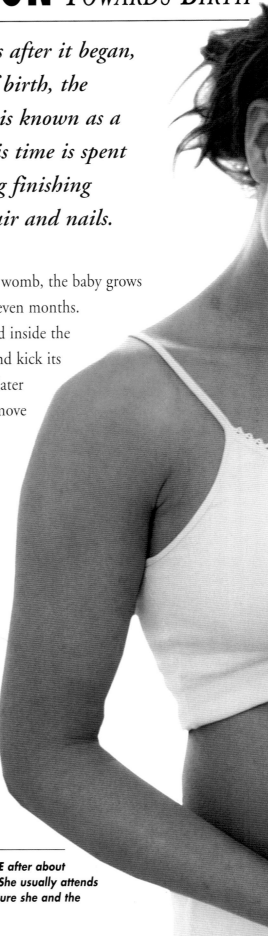

THE MOTHER'S ABDOMEN BEGINS TO BULGE *after about four months of the nine-month pregnancy. She usually attends antenatal ('before birth') checks, to make sure she and the developing baby are well.*

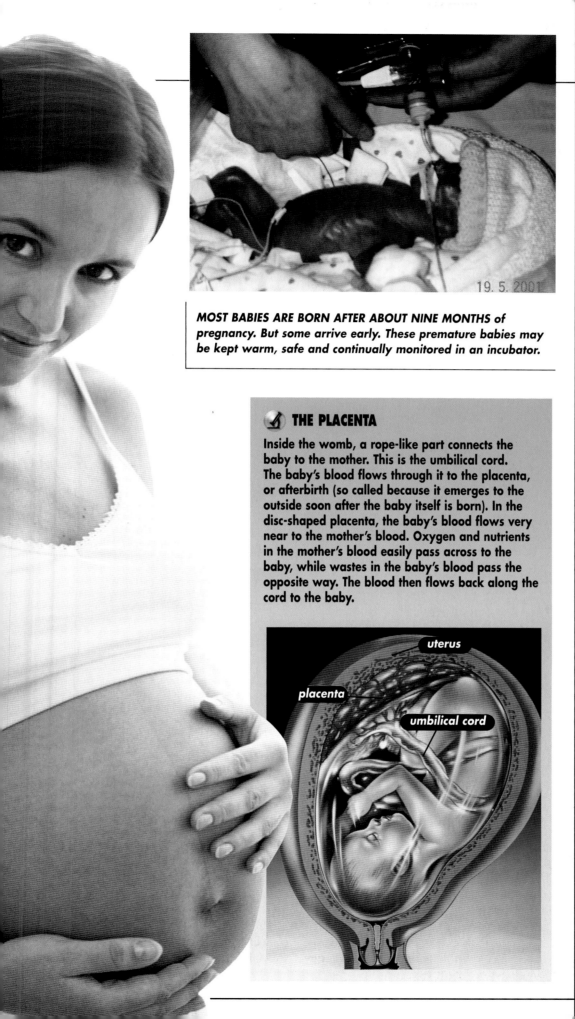

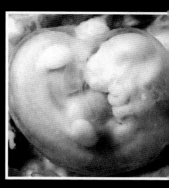

MOST BABIES ARE BORN AFTER ABOUT NINE MONTHS of pregnancy. But some arrive early. These premature babies may be kept warm, safe and continually monitored in an incubator.

After just a few weeks, the fetus starts to take on a human appearance, with hands, feet and head recognisable.

🔬 THE PLACENTA

Inside the womb, a rope-like part connects the baby to the mother. This is the umbilical cord. The baby's blood flows through it to the placenta, or afterbirth (so called because it emerges to the outside soon after the baby itself is born). In the disc-shaped placenta, the baby's blood flows very near to the mother's blood. Oxygen and nutrients in the mother's blood easily pass across to the baby, while wastes in the baby's blood pass the opposite way. The blood then flows back along the cord to the baby.

After several months, the fetus's body becomes tubbier and covered in a creamy substance, vernix, which stops the skin from becoming waterlogged.

uterus

placenta

umbilical cord

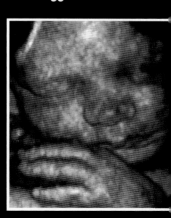

By 8–9 months the fetus is ready to be born. The average weight of a baby at birth is 3–3.5 kg.

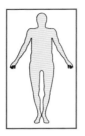

Our knowledge of the body's health, diet, illness and treatment has meant huge advances in the length and quality of our lives.

Children of today are about 2 cm taller, for the same age, than children of 100 years ago.

In most developed countries, the average **lifespan for people born 200 years ago was about 30–35 years**.

REPRODUCTION *Baby to Adult*

Most people do not reach their full body height until about 20 years. Greatest muscle power may occur a few years later. But growing up is not only physical. Also important is how we behave, learn new information, take decisions, make friends and get on with other people.

INFANCY & CHILDHOOD From the moment of birth the new baby learns at an amazing rate. It learns the sounds, sights and smells of its mother and family. From about six weeks it learns that if it smiles, other people smile back and play with it, which is less boring than lying alone. From about five months a typical baby can sit up, then at eight months crawl, and 11–12 months walk. These actions and movements are called motor skills. Most babies develop them in the same order but the ages differ widely.

THE NEWBORN BABY IS NOT ENTIRELY 'HELPLESS'. It has built-in reactions or instincts to cry when hungry, hot, cold, damp or uncomfortable – such as when its nappy needs changing.

FROM THE AGE OF ABOUT TWO, young children want to find out and explore. But they do not understand about danger. This can often lead to a battle of wills which ends in the temper tantrums of the 'terrible twos'.

CHILD TO ADULT At the age of two years, most toddlers are about half as tall as they will be when they are adults. But their weight is only one-fifth of their expected adult weight. During childhood, growth gradually slows down. Then from about 9–12 years in girls, and a couple of years later in boys, growth speeds up again and the body changes in shape and features. The reproductive parts enlarge and begin to work, during the time known as puberty. In boys this takes up to four years, in girls about two or three years.

During the teenage years, many people spend less time with their close family and more with others of their own age. Friendships can become very intense, very fast – then fade just as quickly.

✐ GROWING UP FAST

Until puberty, girls and boys have similar body sizes and outlines. During puberty the average male body grows taller and more angular, with broader shoulders, increased muscle, facial hair (see left) and a much deeper or 'broken' voice. The average female body grows not quite so tall, and becomes more rounded with wider hips, developed breasts, and a slightly deeper voice.

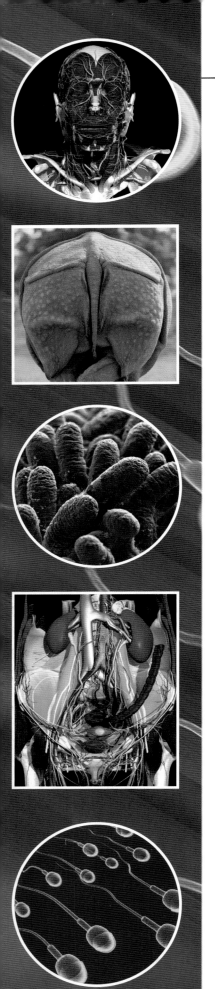

ABDOMEN The lower main body, from the base of the chest down to the hips, which contains the main parts for digestion, waste disposal and reproduction.

ACTIN One of the two main substances in a muscle, shaped as tiny threads, which slides between similar threads of myosin as a muscle shortens.

ALLERGY A bodily process that resembles the defence reaction to harmful germs or toxins, caused by substances like plant pollen grains or house dust.

APPENDIX A small, finger-like, dead-end branch from the start of the large intestine, in the lower right of the abdomen.

ARTERIOLE A type of blood vessel carrying blood away from the heart into organs and tissue, thinner than an artery but not as narrow as a capillary.

ARTERY Strong, thick-walled main blood vessel that carries blood away from the heart. Note: Not all arteries carry bright red, high-oxygen blood. The pulmonary arteries to the lungs convey dark, low-oxygen, 'blue' blood.

ATRIUM One of the two small upper chambers of the heart, which receives blood flowing in from the veins and passes it to the ventricle below.

ATROPHY When a body part such as a muscle is not used regularly and becomes weaker, smaller and 'wasted'.

AUDITORY To do with the sense of hearing, for example, the auditory nerve carries nerve signals from the cochlea deep in the ear, to the brain.

AUTONOMIC NERVOUS SYSTEM Parts of the nerve system which deal with 'automatic' body processes, that we do not have to think about controlling, such as heartbeat and digesting food.

ALVEOLI Microscopic bubble-shaped air sacs in the lungs, where oxygen passes from air into the blood.

AXON The long, wire-like part extending from a nerve cells, also called a nerve fibre, which passes nerve signals onwards to other cell.

BALANCED DIET A suitable selection of varied foods that keeps the body healthy and minimises the risks of various diseases.

BLADDER A bag- or sac-like body part, usually meaning the urinary bladder which stores urine made by the kidneys.

BRAIN STEM The lower, narrower part at the base of the brain, which extends downwards and tapers into the spinal cord. It deals mainly with automatic body processes like the heartbeat.

BRONCHI The larger airways in the chest, which branch from the base of the windpipe (trachea).

BRONCHIOLES Air tubes in the chest, narrower than bronchi but not as thin as terminal bronchioles.

CAPILLARY The thinnest, shortest type of blood vessel, far too narrow to see with the unaided eye.

CALCIUM An important mineral that gives hardness and strength to bones and teeth.

CANCELLOUS BONE The honeycomb-like or spongy bone substance that forms the middle layer of most bones, with compact bone outside it and marrow inside.

CARTILAGE A strong, smooth, shiny, slightly bendy substance, sometimes called 'gristle', that forms body parts like the nose and ears, and covers the ends of bones in a joint.

CELLS Tiny parts or building-blocks of the body, which in their billions make up larger parts like bones, muscles and skin.

CENTRAL NERVOUS SYSTEM The brain and spinal cord.

CEREBELLUM The small, lower rear part of the brain, with a wrinkled surface, which is mainly involved in controlling movements.

CEREBROSPINAL FLUID A liquid found between the innermost (pia mater) and middle (arachnoid) layers of the meninges, around the brain and spinal cord. It helps to cushion and protect the brain.

CEREBRUM The large, upper, domed, wrinkled part of the brain, consisting of two halves, the cerebral hemispheres.

CILIA Tiny hair-like projections of microscopic cells, found in many body parts. Cilia on the smell and taste cells respond to certain chemical substances carrying odours or flavours.

COCHLEA The small, curly, snail-shaped part deep in the ear, which changes sound vibrations into nerve signals.

COLLAGEN A tough, strong substance which forms micro-fibres in the skin and gives it strength, and is also found in other body parts, like tendons.

COLON Another name for most of the large intestine.

COMPACT BONE The hard, dense, very strong bone substance that forms the outer layer or 'shell' of most bones.

CONES Tapering cells in the retina of the eye that sense light rays and colours but work only in bright conditions.

CORTEX The thin, greyish covering of the cerebrum (cerebral hemispheres) – the main part where conscious thinking, awareness, experience of senses and control of muscles occur.

CRANIUM The domed upper part of the skull that covers the brain.

DEHYDRATION Lack of water, which in the body can cause serious problems in just a few hours.

DENTINE A tough substance under the enamel coating of a tooth, resembling the 'ivory' of an elephant tusk.

DIAPHRAGM A large sheet of muscle, shaped like a double-dome, at the base of the chest under the lungs.

DENDRITES Small, spidery-looking, branched parts extending from the main part or body of a nerve cell, which receive nerve signals from other nerve cells.

DERMIS The inner or lower layer of skin, under the epidermis, which contains blood vessels, hair roots and touch sensors.

EEG Electro-encephalogram, a paper tracing or screen display of wavy, spiky lines that represent nerve signals in the brain, detected by sensor pads stuck to the skin of the head and scalp.

ELASTIN A strong, flexible substance that forms micro-fibres in the skin and allows it to bend and stretch.

ENAMEL The whitish or pale yellow covering of a tooth – enamel is the hardest substance in the body.

ENDOCRINE GLAND A hormone-making gland. It does not have a tube or duct to carry away its product, but releases the hormone directly into the blood flowing through the gland.

ENZYMES Substances which speed up or slow down the rate of chemical processes and changes. Digestive enzymes speed the breakdown of food in the stomach and intestines.

EPIDERMIS The outermost or surface layer of skin, which is mostly dead and continually being worn away.

EXCRETION The removal of unwanted substances and wastes from the body.

FOLLICLE The tiny pit or 'pocket' in the skin, from which a hair grows.

GALL BLADDER A small bag behind the liver on the lower right, which stores the fluid bile made by the liver and passes it into the small intestine.

GASTRIC To do with the stomach.

HEPATIC To do with the liver.

HORMONE A natural substance made in the body by an endocrine gland, which circulates in the blood and controls a certain process or change.

INVOLUNTARY MUSCLE The muscle of inner parts like the lung, airways and guts, also called unstriated or visceral muscle, which we cannot control at will.

KERATIN A hard, strong, tough substance found in the outer layer (epidermis) of skin, and which also forms hairs and nails.

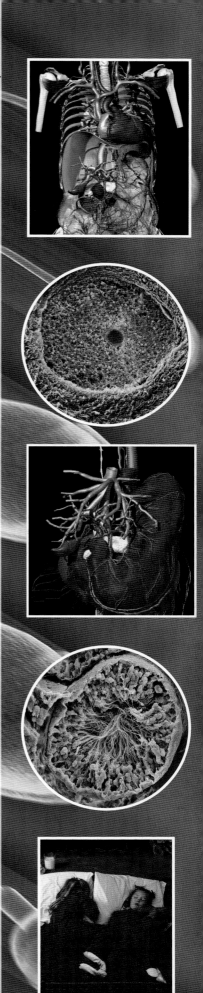

LACTIC ACID A waste product made by active muscles, which is usually taken away by the blood. If it builds up in a muscle it may cause cramp.

LARYNX Name for the voicebox area.

LIGAMENT A strong, slightly stretchy part shaped like a strap or cord, which holds bones together at a joint, allowing them to move to a certain extent but not too much.

MARROW A soft, jelly-like substance inside some bones, which makes new microscopic cells for the blood.

MENINGES Three very thin layers that wrap closely around the brain and spinal cord, and with the cerebrospinal fluid, cushion them from knocks and jolts.

MINERALS Simple substances, many of which are metals in pure form, needed by the body to work well and stay healthy. They include iron, calcium, iodine, sodium and potassium.

MOTOR In the body, to do with muscles and movements, for example, a motor nerve carries nerve signals from the brain out to muscles to control their movements.

MUSCLE A body part specialised to get shorter, or contract.

MYOFIBRES Thin, thread-like parts or muscle fibres that form bundles inside a muscle, and are themselves made of myofibrils (muscle fibrils).

MYOFIBRILS Very thin, thread-like parts or muscle fibrils that form bundles inside a muscle fibre, and are themselves made of strands of actin and myosin.

MYOSIN Protein in muscle cells responsible for the elastic properties of muscles.

NASAL CHAMBERS The air spaces inside the nose, through which air passes as we breathe in and out.

NEPHRONS Tiny filtering units in the kidney which remove unwanted substances and excess water from blood to form urine.

NERVE A long, cord-like body part that carries information in the form of tiny pulses of electricity called nerve signals.

NEURON A nerve cell specially designed in shape to receive and pass on nerve signals.

OLFACTORY To do with the sense of smell, for example, the olfactory epithelium is the 'smell patch' inside the nose where odours are detected.

OSSIFICATION The process by which the parts of the skeleton formed first as substance cartilage, which then gradually changes in babies and children, into harder, stronger bone.

OSTEONS The building-blocks of bones, each made of the substance collagen hardened with crystals of minerals, which are shaped like tiny rods and jammed together in bundles.

OXYGEN A gas with no colour, taste or smell, that makes up one-fifth of air. It is needed by the body to release the energy from food substances, especially blood sugar or glucose.

PAPILLAE On the tongue, the small but visible lumps and 'pimples' that give it a rough surface and house the much smaller tastes buds.

PERISTALSIS Moving waves or constrictions of muscles along a tube-like body part, squeezing along its contents, such as food in the gut or urine in the ureter.

PERIPHERAL NERVOUS SYSTEM The system of nerves that branch from the brain and spinal cord.

PERSPIRATION To produce the watery liquid sweat from sweat glands, which draws heat from the body as it dries on the surface of skin.

PHARYNX Name for the throat area. (A sore throat is known as pharyngitis.)

PLAQUE In blood vessels, a lump of fatty substance that forms in the lining, like 'fur' in a water pipe, and which narrows or even blocks the vessel.

PLEURAE Smooth, slippery, bag-like layers that wrap around the lungs and allow them to change size with the movements of breathing.

RETINA The very thin inner lining of the eyeball, which changes patterns of light rays into nerve signals.

RESPIRATION 1: For the whole body, breathing air in and out to obtain oxygen and get rid of carbon dioxide. 2: In a cell, the chemical breakdown of blood sugar or glucose, using oxygen, to release its energy (cellular respiration).

RENAL To do with the kidneys.

RODS Tall, rounded cells in the retina of the eye, which sense light rays and work in dim conditions but do not detect colours.

SEBACEOUS GLANDS Tiny glands in the skin, each next to a hair, which make natural oils and waxes to keep skin supple and water-repellent.

SINUSES Honeycomb-like air spaces within the skull bones around the face, connected to the main airway in the nose by openings or ducts.

SKELETON The body's bone structure, plus various supporting parts which are made mainly of cartilage.

SPINAL CORD The main nerve extending from the base of the brain, along the inside the backbone (spinal column).

SPINAL NERVES Nerves that branch off the spinal cord, between the individual bones or vertebrae of the backbone (spinal column).

STRIPED MUSCLE The muscle which is attached to bones, also called striated or skeletal muscle, and which we can control at will to move (voluntary muscle).

SUTURE In the skeleton, a place where two bones are joined together firmly and cannot move, usually visible as a faint wiggly line.

SYNOVIAL FLUID A thick, slippery liquid inside most joints, which works like lubricating oil to make movements smoother and reduce wear.

TASTE BUD A tiny cluster of cells, far too small to seen, that detects tastes.

TENDON The strong, rope-like part where a muscle tapers or becomes narrower and is fixed to a bone (or to another muscle).

TERMINAL BRONCHIOLES The thinnest air tubes in the lungs, which end at groups of microscopic air sacs, alveoli.

THORAX The chest region, from the neck and shoulders down to the abdomen, which contains the heart and main blood vessels, and the lungs and main airways.

TRACHEA Name for the windpipe, extending from the base of the voicebox (larynx) down to the site where it branches into two smaller airways, the bronchi.

UNSTRIPED MUSCLE The muscle of inner parts like the guts, also called unstriated or visceral muscle, which we cannot control at will (involuntary muscle).

VENTRICLE One of the two large lower chambers of the heart, which receives blood flowing into it from the atrium above, and pumps it out into the arteries.

VENULE A type of blood vessel carrying blood from organs and tissues towards the heart, wider than a capillary but not as large as a vein.

VERTEBRAE The individual bones which make up the body's backbone or spinal column.

VOCAL CORDS Small flaps or ridges in the voicebox, which shake very fast or vibrate to make the sounds of the voice.

UMBILICAL CORD The rope-like part linking the unborn baby to the placenta or afterbirth in the wall of the womb.

URETER Tube conveying urine from the kidney to the bladder.

URETHRA Tube conveying urine from the bladder to the outside.

UTERUS The womb, the female reproductive part where a baby grows and develops before birth.

VEIN Wide but thin-walled main blood vessel that carries blood back to the heart. Note: Not all veins
carry dark, low-oxygen 'blue' blood. The umbilical vein from the placenta to the unborn baby conveys bright red, high-oxygen blood.

VITAMINS Substances needed in small amounts for the body to stay healthy and work well. Many are found in fresh fruits and vegetables, and some, such as vitamin D, can be made by the body.

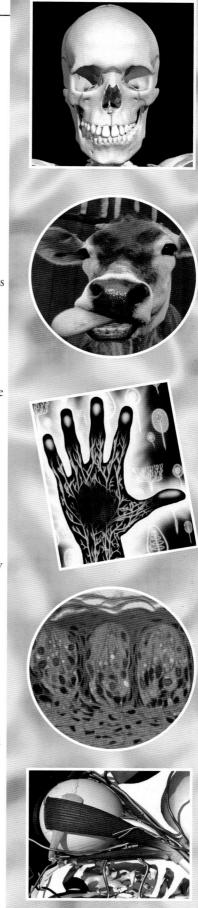

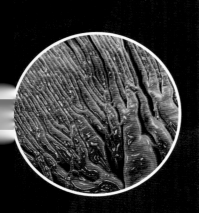

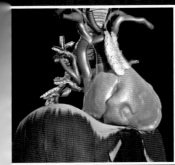

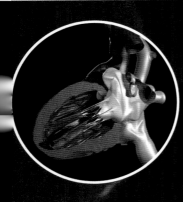

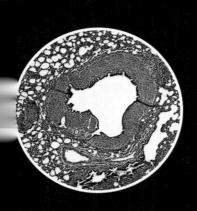

I N D E X

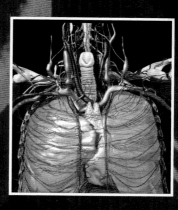
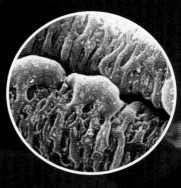
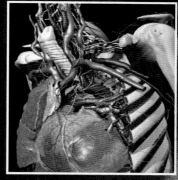
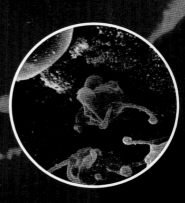
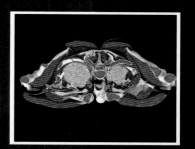

ACKNOWLEDGMENTS

Copyright © ticktock Entertainment Ltd 2005
First published in Great Britain in 2005 by ticktock Media Ltd.,
Unit 2, Orchard Business Centre, North Farm Road, Tunbridge Wells, Kent, TN2 3XF
We would like to thank: Elizabeth Wiggans and Jenni Rainford for their help with this book.
ISBN 1 86007 564 9
Printed in China
A CIP catalogue record for this book is available from the British Library.

Picture Credits:
Alamy: OFCl, 8, 6r, 9r, 11b, 16-17c, 20-21c, 30-31, 32r, 44-45, 50-51c, 52-53c, 57t & br, 59b, 67c, 74-75c, 86-87c. *Mediscan*: 11 tr & cr, 51cr,
55tr, 64-65c, 90-91c, 92-93c. *Primal Pictures*: 4, 7 all, 18r, 19l & tr & cr, 21tr & cr, 23c & tr & cr, 25r all, 27tr & cr, 29tr & cr, 31r all & b, 35tr,
39tr, 43tr & cr, 45tr & cr, 47 tr & cr, 53tr, 59tr, 61tr, 63tr, 65tr, 67tr, 69tr, 71tr, 72-73c, 73tr & cr, 75tr, 79tr, 81tr & cr, 83r, 89tr, 91tr & cr,
92t, 93tr & cr, 95tr, 97tr & cr. *Science Photo Library*: 2, 8, 9l, 12-13c, 15tr & cr, 17tr & cr, 23t, 29b, 32b, 35br, 38-39c, 39cr, 40tl, 41cb,
49tr & cr, 53r, 61br, 71c, 73t, 75cr, 78tl, 79t, 81br, 83b, 88t, 91br, 94-95c, 95br, 99b, 193b. *Wellcome Trust*: 101r all, 103 tr & br.